# BEGINNERS GUIDE

## SPACE

*Learn how to start Cricut, Step by Step learning for Design Space, Cricut Project Ideas*

**By**
**Richard Reedy**

© **Copyright 2020 by Richard Reedy - All rights reserved.**

This document is geared towards providing exact and reliable information in regards to the topic and issue covered. The publication is sold with the idea that the publisher is not required to render accounting, officially permitted, or otherwise, qualified services. If advice is necessary, legal or professional, a practiced individual in the profession should be ordered.

- From a Declaration of Principles which was accepted and approved equally by a Committee of the American Bar Association and a Committee of Publishers and Associations.

In no way is it legal to reproduce, duplicate, or transmit any part of this document in either electronic means or in printed format. Recording of this publication is strictly prohibited and any storage of this document is not allowed unless with written permission from the publisher. All rights reserved.

The information provided herein is stated to be truthful and consistent, in that any liability, in terms of inattention or otherwise, by any usage or abuse of any policies, processes, or directions contained within is the solitary and utter responsibility of the recipient reader. Under no circumstances will any legal responsibility or blame be held against the publisher for any reparation, damages, or monetary loss due to the information herein, either directly or indirectly.

Respective authors own all copyrights not held by the publisher.

The information herein is offered for informational purposes solely, and is universal as so. The presentation of the information is without contract or any type of guarantee assurance.

The trademarks that are used are without any consent, and the publication of the trademark is without permission or backing by the trademark owner. All trademarks and brands within this book are for clarifying purposes only and are the owned by the owners themselves, not affiliated with this document.

# Table of contents

**INTRODUCTION** ........................................................................... 6

**CHAPTER 1: INTRODUCTION TO CRICUT AND ITS USAGE** ............................................................................................ 8

1.1: What is Cricut?.................................................................................8

1.2: Components of Cricut ....................................................................9

1.3: Why should you use Cricut? .......................................................10

1.4: Choosing the right Cricut model ................................................12

1.5: Setting up the Cricut machine ....................................................16

1.6: Which tools to start with? ...........................................................17

**CHAPTER 2: WHAT IS CRICUT DESIGN SPACE AND WHY SHOULD YOU START?** ................................................... 21

2.1: Introduction to Cricut design space ..........................................21

2.2: Cricut Access subscription .........................................................22

2.3: How Design Space helps use Cricut even with no experience ...........24

2.4: Getting started with Cricut Design Space Software ...............27

**CHAPTER 3: WORKING WITH CRICUT DESIGN SPACE** ........................................................................................................32

3.1: Getting the machine ready .........................................................32

3.2: Configuring the Cricut Design Space........................................39

3.3: Using PDF Files in Cricut Design Space...................................44

3.4: Your first design with the Cricut design space .................................................. 55

3.5: Turning your design dreams into reality ................................................. 57

## CHAPTER 4: MATERIALS & ACCESSORIES FOR WORKING WITH CRICUT .......................................................... 66

4.1: Which materials the Cricut machines can cut? ....................................... 66

4.2: What the Cricut machines can craft? ......................................................... 68

4.3: Essentials for working with Cricut ............................................................. 71

## CHAPTER 5: CREATIVE CRICUT PROJECT IDEAS .......... 82

5.1: Project ideas for beginners ......................................................................... 82

5.2: Project ideas for advanced level ................................................................. 96

5.3: Business ideas for making money with Cricut ..................................... 107

## CHAPTER 6: MAINTAINING CRICUT AND TIPS FOR ITS EFFECTIVE USE ........................................................................ 109

6.1: How to maintain your Cricut machine .................................................... 109

6.2: Tips and tricks for cost and time efficiency ........................................... 114

## CHAPTER 7: FREQUENTLY ASKED QUESTIONS .......... 120

7.1: FAQs ............................................................................................................... 120

## CONCLUSION ............................................................................. 126

## REFERENCES ............................................................................. 128

# Introduction

Cricut is a material design and cutting system which is specifically known as a die-cutting machine. It allows you to do numerous DIY projects like cards, invitations, vinyl designs, and much more. No matter what creative idea you might have, with the help of Cricut, you can probably do it. Cricut is a die-cutting machine that resembles a printer that has cutters attached to it. It can be used for printing and cutting of various materials. So if you wonder what a Cricut machine is? A suitable response is that it is a home die-cutting machine used to create paper and various crafts and arts. It is basically an excellent cutting machine known as "the perfect entry point to the exact crafting universe." In fact, it is an artisan's companion who gives you the freedom to create amazing designs for different occasions. Many people think that these machines just cut paper, but they can do so much more than just cutting paper.

Cricut offers free online software called Cricut design space to let you put your ideas out into the world. You can create your projects using this software. You need not worry about your machine because this software works with all the modern Cricut machines. If you have never used Cricut design space but want to know how you can start your projects and create great designs in no time at all, you have come to the right place. You can do it with all modern Cricut machines using the Cricut design space. This guide will show you all you need to know, and finally, it will allow you to make full use of your creativity.

This guide will cover two main parts - The machine and the Design space software, respectively. It may seem like too much information at first, but there's no need to get worried, You'll get used to it after a short time and see how all the systems work together. This guide will help you get a concise overview of your tasks and will encourage you to come up with fresh and innovative ideas. With a little practice, it should become effortless to use this machine and the design space program. You will take a closer look at some of the core features in the second section. You will also understand individual interface attributes and how they interact.

This guide is specifically directed towards beginners. Also, if some information sometimes seems obvious, please note that the user experience can differ. This guide should be accessible and easy to understand to everyone willing to learn. That way, any guesswork will be eliminated, and you can emerge from this experience with a solid foundation in Cricut Design space.

# Chapter 1: Introduction to Cricut and its usage

For Cricut, the generic title is a die cutter, craft plotter, or smart cutter machine. This machine's format allows you to build projects from flat materials of varying densities. Depending on your skill level with these materials, the productions you can do with this machine can range from simple to moderately complex. Your materials can range from craft felt to thin sheets of metal, depending on the sharpness of the blade in your cutting machine, or the model you are using and thus giving you an outlook of how broad the range is for what this machine can enable you to achieve as a crafter.

## 1.1: What is Cricut?

Many people have heard of a Cricut machine, and because of everything you can do with it, it's been making a big splash in the crafting world. You might be surprised to be able to work with a lot of different materials on this machine, and it can be an entertaining way of making some exceptional items.

You needed cartridges when Cricut machines first came out to be able to cut your letters and the shapes you wanted to use for your items, but now you don't need cartridges at all! Today this is done digitally, and everyone knows we have amazing technology at our feet, and we can use it to our favor.

Most Cricut machines can now work over Bluetooth or Wi-Fi, which means you can design on your iPad, or you can also use this if you have an iPhone. You can use this from your computer, too. This makes it easier than ever to design your passions, and you have complete versatility to help you do what you want, and to have flexible options at your disposal.

Other machines of this kind can cost you several hundred or even thousands of dollars, require design degrees, come with complex proprietary software, and offer only a fraction of Cricut's design choices, as well as the proprietary, user-friendly Cricut Design Space. In projects, tips, tricks, tutorials and new tools to use for your Cricut tool, Cricut's massive user base is always sharing the latest and greatest. For a Cricut machine crafter, the opportunities are almost infinite.

As just like many other crafting outlets, if you don't pay attention, you may spend more on supplies, equipment, accessories and more than you anticipated. The aim is to show you which proprietary tools are worth the extra money, while at the same time showing you the best alternatives you can use in place of others. Crafting is such a therapeutic and pleasant experience; thanks to the cost, this should not be prohibitive! When you become acquainted with the Cricut user community, and the Cricut brand, You'll surely find the tools and tricks that work best for you to bring your crafts to life!

## 1.2 : Components of Cricut

The Cricut machines, the Cricut Explore Air, the Cricut Explore Air one, and the Cricut Explore Air 2, are the four most common models. You should be aware that every Cricut machine has similar items like what they come with. The following components are used in all machines.

- Project supplies
- Power adjuster
- Access to free projects ready to manufacture
- A mat that is 12 inches by 12 inches

You should also know that some models have extra items, exclusive writing styles, different blades or even wheels.

## 1.3: Why should you use Cricut?

So now that you know what the machine is, we're going to tell you what it does and why it's so incredible. So let's kick-off. When you use your desktop or smartphone, whatever type you want to use for this, it can connect to your machine and then submit to your cutting machine whatever configuration you want. The design is going to indicate what it needs, meaning to be graded or cut if it requires a brush. The machine then is going to do the rest for you.

Every machine has its own branded software. Using and uploading it into or onto your computer is free. Cricut also comes with an app that you can use. The software is user friendly, and you can upload photos and build designs. You can make your designs from scratch, or buy other designs. You can also upload images from the application and buy designs and change them to match your custom designs.

Cricut Design Space is a cloud-based framework. Therefore, to make the most of the application for your designs, you need a robust high-Speed Internet connection. The cloud functionality also allows you the access to your account, your designs, your apps and anything inside the design room, from any computer anywhere in the world as long as you have your credentials and are connected to the internet

The app is easy to use, and while it's easy to use, the app is straightforward. It gives you the capability to develop your projects. The app will You'll tell your machine where your scoring or writing needs to take place. It also indicates you where to cut.

The computer will render a complete design if only one step is required. However, if there are multiple steps, the device you have connected to your machine will convey this to you. It will just tell you If you need more steps.

The Maker version is available in three colors, while the Explore series is available in several others, but they are both exceptional. The first in the explore series is the basic system that operates since it is also the most affordable. It can cost over $300 depending on what you want to do. Their latest model is the Explore Air 2. As such, it has more features and functionality and the highest machine price.

The Maker is the only one with an adaptive tool system for your advantage and is said to have more flexibility than other ones. It is also unique because you have a toolkit that will provide you with more materials than ever. It also has a technology that regulates the direction and the pressure of your blade by rolling. This means that you can work much better with your stuff.

You now know the basics and also what a Cricut does. Now your concern is probably what types of projects or designs you might do with them. We shall address this in this book later, as you can actually use it in hundreds of different ways. The capacitive stylus support designs as well. Such a machine uses many devices for various purposes and tasks, and it is good to have your machine do exactly what you want.

A machine like this will not actually be a printer, but it can be that it comes close. If you use the "print, then cut" method, it will allow you to design your project and take it from there so that you can use it properly. It would be a little like making stickers if you want to think about it.

It also cuts materials other than paper. These machines no longer represent only die-hard scrapbookers. It does so much more. This book contains a master list of all the functions of your machine and how to get the most out of it.

## 1.4: Choosing the right Cricut model

The best thing about Cricut is that they all have incredibly flexible and capable models. Most capabilities one model has could cover the entire current Cricut product line. There are some very minor variations in how they operate and the nature of their activity. We've listed all the models currently available from Cricut in the section below, what they do, how they vary, and what areas are better among specific models

**What are the options?**

Luckily, at the time of writing, there aren't a vast number of craft plotters available from Cricut, which means it'll be pretty quick for you to take a look at all the options without becoming overwhelmed. With huge product lines that contain many different models, it can be a real chore to find what you want and need while getting the most for your money. Each of the currently available versions, what they can do, and the characteristics ideally suited to what types of crafts are outlined in this chapter.

**Cricut Explore One**

This is the simplest machine they sell, in terms of what's typically available from Cricut. This machine promises the ability to cut 100 of the most common materials presently available for use with your Cricut machine and is also extremely user friendly.

The Cricut Explore One is regarded by Cricut craft plotters as the no-frills beginner model and runs at a slower speed than the other available versions. The Cricut Explore One has just one component clamp within, so cutting or scoring can't be performed simultaneously, as compared to the others found in the current model line. Nevertheless, they can be performed in quick succession, one right after the other.

While this is a fantastic tool for a wide variety of crafts on 100 different materials and will get you on the right track to create beautiful crafts that are often cut from others, the cost is not as high as you would think. If you're going to use your art plotter mainly for those special occasions where almost everything crafted is perfect, then this is a fantastic tool to have on hand.

## Cricut Explore Air

With all of the features of the Cricut Explore One and More capabilities, the Cricut Explore Air model comes loaded with Bluetooth functionality, has an integrated-in storage container to hold your tools in one place while you're working, so they won't roll away or get lost in the shuffle.

This model does have two on-board accessory clamps which allow for marking and cutting or scoring simultaneously. These clamps are labeled with an A and a B, so each time you load them up, you can be confident that your tools are going in the right positions.

This model is designed to handle the same 100 materials as the Cricut Explore One and runs at the same pace, so the difference in price represents individual variations and similarities! This is a fantastic deal you're getting for the powerhouse.

## Cricut Explore Air 2

The Cricut Explore Air 2 is the current top-selling craft plotter from Cricut and is probably the best value they can give for the price. Each model cuts materials twice the speed of both the previous ones; this model has Bluetooth support and two adapter clamps on board.

The storage cup at the top of the unit features a smaller, shallower cut to hold your replacement blade housings while they aren't in use. If you want to swap for a project between several different tips, they're all readily accessible in your task.

All cups have a smooth silicone rim, so you won't have to worry about your blades getting rusty or scratched

It is the perfect tool for the job for someone who finds themselves using their Cricut with some frequency. You will be able to do your crafts twice as quickly, and each time, even at that pace, you will get a favorable outcome!

**The Cricut Maker**

The Cricut Maker is known as the flagship model of Cricut. It's the one that can do almost anything under the sun on almost any content you can bring into your machine's mat guides. The price point is the only drawback of this powerhouse model, and Unless you want to make crafts that this model will sell, this model proves to be quite expensive. So when you are determined, you can be confident that whatever you do with this machine will always be the cream of the crop. This baby is going to pay for itself in a short time if you sell your crafts.

This machine may be full to capacity for the enthusiastic crafters who want to turn up at the party with the most exquisite creations, that are ahead of their colleagues. Of course, this is the pattern you would have if you're keeping up with the Joneses.

This model has everything, and we will explain it. There is no other Cricut machine with the speed of the Cricut Maker. The cuts that can be made using the precise blades that just fit this machine are more smooth than anything from a straight knife or other craft cutters you could ever expect. You can easily remove the tip from the housing using blade housings, add the next one, clip it back into place and start to roll your designs. Moreover, the machine will identify the loaded material, so at the start of the project, you won't have to specify the type of material. One common problem in the other model is that the project is completed halfway before the crafter discovers that the dial has been wrongly specified.

The machine is, as some other models, fully Bluetooth compatible, 10 times more potent than any other, it has a specialized rotary cutter attachment that allows it to glide effortlessly through fabrics with accuracy and much more.

**Outdated Models**

Some old models for Explore and Maker devices are slowly being terminated. 1 The older machines needed a lot more tricks, operating processes, troubleshooting and understanding to get precision or even cuts for the projects craftsmen would want to do.

Here are some of the models which have been outdated.

Cricut Create

Expression 1

Expression 2

Imagine

Cricut Mini

These models were compatible with a Cricut device called the Gypsy, not the same as the Cricut Design Space currently in use today. Each machine has triumphed in innovating the processes of handcraft cutting.

Cricut's main goal was to amend the complexity of operating with its machinery while creating its newest line of models. Crafter groups had exchanged hacks and mathematical leads to plan their machines precisely as they wanted it to.

The new selection of models available allows you to be imaginative as possible in the design process so that no operations that your computer can take care of are taken up in your creative flow.

When you own one of these machines, it needs upgrading, but you don't need to upgrade if you've done your crafting well with the one you have on hand. Cricut has always created products of superior quality, and Cricut Design Space still supports cartridges containing various thematic design elements.

Cricut Cartridge Adapter is a USB adapter that enables the import of your cartridges into Cricut design space so that all your elements are accessible in an organized place.

## 1.5: Setting up the Cricut machine

There are various platforms you can use to set up your Cricut system, including the Windows / Mac and iOS / Android systems. The steps to set up your Cricut machine using either of the platforms, depending on which one you have are described briefly below:

For Windows / Mac:

1. Plug your cricut machine using the power outlet

2. Power ON your Cricut machine Connect your device and your Cricut machine using the USB cable, connect via Bluetooth otherwise. Build your Cricut ID or sign in to design space platform if you already have one.

3. When you're prompted to do so, download the Design Space plugin.

4. Install the Design Space on your Computer. The plugin Design Space is super easy to download and install. It's when you're asked to launch your first project you know that your setup process is done.

For iOS / Android

1. To plug your Cricut machine, use the power outlet.

2. Power ON Your Cricut machine.

3. Connect your Cricut machine with your iOS or Android device via Bluetooth

4. Download and install the Design Space plugin.

5. Start the downloaded app Build a Cricut ID to sign in and if you already have one, use it to sign in.

6. Click on menu and tap System Setup and App Description Tap New Machine Setup. Follow the on-screen instructions to complete the setup.

7. Again, you know that your setup process is complete is when you're prompted to begin your first project.

The detailed procedures for connecting the Cricut Machine to the Cricut Design Space Apps will be discussed in the next chapter. You'll also learn to use the cricut design space interface in detail in the next chapter along with the basics of Cricut Design Space.

## 1.6: Which tools to start with?

Cricut is a brand responsive to its clients. Through this, they have thought of every tool that you may need to complete your project right from the start. Mentioned below is a list of all tools that will help you get the projects out and into practice in Cricut Design Space.

Look at these things, get an idea of what they are, what they do, and see some of them right off the bat that can be replaced by other items that don't belong to the Cricut brand.

You can save money in doing this and may use some of the tools that you have around your crafting station right now! Let's dive in.

**Bonded Fabric Blades**

These blades are made of German carbide steel for simple and precise cutting through bonded cloth. With the FabricGrip™ pad, they can be used to hold the fabric in place for the most accurate, smoothest cuts.

These blades, and the adapters that are also available for them, are specially designed and built to suit the Cricut cutting machines Explore line, including the Explore Air models. The Cricut Maker needs a special kind of blade and space.

## Craft Tweezers

Upon extended use, these reverse-action tweezers have a good grip, precise points and relieve cramping. h The ergonomic grip helps maintain a firm hold on the materials during the whole process, giving the crafter extra pair of hands he'd always wish he had while crafting

## Cricut Explore ® Wireless Bluetooth ® Adapter

This product lets you connect your Cricut Explore machine to your computer or smartphone with Bluetooth. If you've invested in the Cricut Explore One but found the Bluetooth capabilities helpful, this handy adapter makes adding that capability to your Cricut Explore One machine easy to work with.

## Deep-point Replacement Blades

Deep-point blades allow you to easily make deeper, more precise cuts to even thicker materials. With time, you may notice the blades in accessory clamp B starting to get dull or only becoming less accurate. To resolve this, Cricut offers a line of substitute blades, and your blades will also adjust to sharpening a few times before replacement.

## Paper Crafting Set

You may find the edge distresser, quilling tool, piercing tool, and craft mat in this collection to be important in your crafts if you're really into paper crafting. Quilling or paper filigree art is nowadays more prevalent than ever, and these are some of the best resources around for that craft.

## Portable Trimmer

This is a precision cutting tool that helps you to cut your projects easily, crisply, and straight almost every time. They are particularly common amongst scrapbookers, and many variations of this product are also on the market, so keep your eye out for those with positive customer reviews and a low price point.

### Replacement Blades

There are replacement blades and housings on the current Cricut line, which are available for each model. All blades that suit the Cricut Explore One can suit into the Cricut Explore line to any configuration. The blades for the Cricut Maker will suit for a particular model, so be sure to review the product details or packaging to make sure you have the perfect blade for yourself.

### Rotary Cutting Kit

This package comes with a grid cutting mat and a rotary cutting tool that cuts quickly and accurately every time. Cricut is far from the only manufacturer that sells a rotary cutting machine, so be sure to look at the product and price that's right for you in other brands on the market.

### Scissors

Every crafter knows scissors are part and parcel of their tool kit. Although the scissors provided by Cricut are exceptionally sharp, with fine dots on each blade, any pair suitable for your craft will serve you well here.

### Scoring Stylus

The scoring stylus is meant to fit perfectly into your machine's accessory clamp A to score your projects for creating and embossing impact, folding lines, and so much more. The tool can also be used creatively to produce the effects you would like to produce in your artwork.

### Scraper / Burnishing Tool

This primary tool would be the most-used Cricut tool, except for the weeding tool. You will find that once you raise your cut designs from the back layer, it will take gentle, steady pressure to furnish your projects beautifully and move them to your project board. This tool can be replaced with other stuff in a pinch, but this tool does the best possible job.

## Spatula

Occasionally when you're peeling or setting down a project, you feel like you need an extra pair of hands. This tool gives you the extra support and controllability you need.

## TrueControl™ Knife

This is a precision blade, similar in price and style to XACTO. This knife is beneficial for more accurate freehand cuts at any carving platform.

## Weeding Tool

This is a very fine point hook that helps you to strip the blanks from the vinyl you cut. For most, if not all, the projects that you do with your Cricut, this device will work wonders. It lets you remove the excess material from your design without bending, folding, or struggling with your stuff. It helps keep the template edges smooth, clean, and sharp whenever you like.

## XL Scraper / Burnishing Tool

It offers a controlled degree, which cannot be beaten. This tool exerts more pressure and helps remove uneven layering and bubbles in the air. The user community highly recommends this tool.

# Chapter 2: What is Cricut design space and why should you start?

Cricut provides an online platform to its users so that they may utilize their creativity to the best. The platform is known as Cricut Design Space, where the actual magic happens before you cut your projects. Here the users can design anything that comes to their mind. The Cricut design space allows the craftsmen to virtually design anything with no limits to their creativity and hence producing extraordinary results.

## 2.1: Introduction to Cricut design space

Design space is cloud-based, meaning you can project and still access your files from anywhere on your computer or mobile device. Start a project on one system and finish without breaking phase on another. You can even download whole plans to use offline on your iOS device, even when there is no internet service available.

You can touch-up and arrange your creations in the Design Space. Not only can you use and upload your fonts and images in this room, but you can also use the premium images and fonts from Cricut through individual purchases, Cricut Access, and Cartridges. The Cricut Design Space Program is entirely web-based technology. You need an active Internet connection for this purpose, but you can hop in and use the Cricut Design Space from the computer by downloading the plug-in. This app can be downloaded to any laptop or tablet and accessed with your credentials, from anywhere, as long as you have an active internet connection

When you log into Cricut Design Space for the first time, the prompts will ask you what sort of Cricut system you would like to use. This will allow the software to interact appropriately with your computer, and correctly lay out your cuts. When you have completed this process, and your machine has found the appropriate system, you may want to click on the "New Project" option in the top right corner. There you will be prompted to download the Cricut Design Space Plugin.

## 2.2: Cricut Access subscription

Cricut offers Cricut Access to get the most out of the library, including several exclusive ones. A monthly or an annual membership plan is provided, which gives you unlimited access to tens of thousands of photos, fonts, and projects. Members enjoy exclusive discounts as well as other incentives on Cricut services

Once you first open the Design Space Plugin Installer, you will be prompted to connect your computer to the Cricut machine. Establishing this link lets you interact seamlessly with your computer and your Cricut machine. When that link is created, you can create projects whenever you want. This means you can import images you've found anywhere, images you've created yourself, or use the photos Cricut provides either free of charge or via Cricut's paid Access subscription.

The first thing to know about Cricut Access is that you don't need Cricut Design Space to use this plan. You can use any part of your Cricut machine without having to sign up for Cricut Access at all.

You can access more than 25,000 images and 200 text types and fonts from your free preliminary access to the Cricut image library. No surprises or credit cards are required, and you simply use your Cricut library to access all authorized photos.

The benefits one gets from a Cricut Access membership vary depending on the tier they want to apply to. At the time of writing, the Cricut Access program has three levels of membership available.

## Monthly-$ 9.99 a month

With a monthly subscription to Cricut Access, you are given unlimited usage of more than 400 fonts available in the Cricut Design Room, boundless, free use of more than 90,000 photos that you can use for any design in the Cricut Design Space, 10 percent member discounts on purchases from Cricut's website, including products already on sale, as well as other things already on sale.

## Annual-$ 7.99 a month (billed once a year at $95.88)

With the annual Cricut Access membership, you are allowed unlimited use of more than 400 fonts available in the Cricut Design Space, boundless, free use of more than 90,000 images that you can use for any Cricut Design Space design, 10 percent member discounts on purchases from Cricut's website, including products that you can use for any Cricut Design Space design Those are all included in the subscription service's annual rate, plus they've added access to a Priority Member Support Line, which cuts customer care wait times in half.

## Premium-$ 9.99 a month (billed once a year at $119.88)

With the premium Cricut Access subscription, you are allowed unlimited use of more than 400 fonts available in the Cricut Design Room, unrestricted, free use of more than 90,000 images that you can use for any Cricut Design Room design, 10 percent member discount on purchases from Cricut's website, including that. With your introductory offer, those are accessible. You also get up to 50 percent discounts on approved fonts, images, and ready-to-make designs, and free economy shipping on all orders from Cricut's website, over $50.

Such member advantages can be useful if you will be doing a lot of projects in a short period. Again, users are by no means required to be members of Access to enjoy the benefits of the Cricut Design Space or its user-friendly user interface. Still, these are the substantial benefits that you can obtain if you register for membership.

## 2.3: How Design Space helps use Cricut even with no experience

Design space is the free layout framework that is at the heart of the functionality of Cricut. For people new to crafting, design space was made easy, but still with enough power for the most experienced crafters.

Cricut Design Space assists you in getting your crafting tasks done without any hassle. You don't need a crafter's experience to start crafting with Cricut. Whether you like making things from scratch or starting with something already designed, your Cricut machine and space design software work together to make the crafting easy. Use the materials in the box to complete your first project and watch how your Cricut machine writes and cuts everything in a single step.

**Library**

In the design room, the Cricut library is full of templates and concepts to ignite your masterpiece. Choose among thousands of images, fonts, and ready-to-make projects to access and operate, all available for instant usage. You will nevertheless find something unique, innovative and inspiring every time as Cricut keeps adding more all the time

**Templates available to render**

Ready to make projects in design space seem to be ideal when you are in a mood to pick something out and get started. Hundreds and thousands of ideas are available to choose from, complete with cut-ready designs, instructions, and lists of materials. All you need to do is follow along.

**Custom design projects**

Designing a project from scratch is an excellent way of experimenting, learning, and expressing your creativity. Design space kick-starts your creative process with hundreds and thousands of images and fonts which you can use as building blocks. Play with them to the content of your heart because the possibilities never end.

**Designing**

You'll arrive on the canvas when you set up a new project, where you lay out your design. Take images from the library (pre-designed, cut-ready shapes) and fonts, then edit, align, color, and resize these components until you have a structure that you like to.

**Making**

Choose your preferred materials, and design space will suggest the right tools for the job (such as blades and ink cartridges). When asked, mount your tools and mats, and the machine takes it from there. When done, remove the cuts carefully from the mats, and you are ready to assemble.

**Preparing mats**

Cricut machine cuts and writes on materials that you put on adhesive mats. Throughout this phase, your designs are arranged per color automatically on mats. For example, red shapes would be placed on the mat holding your red stuff.

**Images in design space**

Images are design aspects configured for rapid and accurate cutting on Cricut machines. The photos in the Cricut library are diverse and impressive, with designs that range from sophisticated to simple, classical to futuristic, formal to whimsical. You can also upload your pictures and photos and then use them, just use the upload option. Design space is compatible with several standard format image files (like .svg, .jpg, .gif, .png, .dxf, .bmp).

**The Cricut library has three image sources**

Cricut images are unique designs created by their creative team. Thousands of images, including both free and premium images, are accessible. The members of Cricut Access enjoy unrestricted use of all premium Cricut images.

In collaboration with top designers like Anna Griffin, designer images are created. These designs are available individually and in sets for purchase so that the users can enhance their crafts with these images.

Licensed images belong to designs and characters of brands such as Disney, Hello Kitty, and Marvel. They are also available separately and in sets for purchase.

The use of premium, designer, or licensed images to display or link to your design is always free. Add as many pictures as you want to the canvas, and make sure to edit or erase them. You will pay only for those you actually use in your project.

**Fonts:**

The Cricut library provides thousands of fonts, all developed to be cut or written using Cricut machines in a broad spectrum of different styles. Like images, a mix of free and premium original fonts comprise Cricut fonts. Members of Cricut Access get unrestricted access to all premium Cricut fonts. Designer fonts and licensed fonts provide you with far more possibilities. The system fonts loaded on your computer or mobile device are almost always accessible.

**The library contains two types of fonts:**

Image fonts can be cut with a blade or drawn with ink, much like images. Most have more than one layer so you can add color, outline, or shadow instantly.

Writing fonts produce letters with a line, in much the same way as you would. It's an exclusive, seamless handwritten effect that sets apart your projects. Many fonts come in both image and writing formats, just like images, before you commit to a purchase, you can play with any premium, designer, or licensed font on your canvas.

The detailed procedures for connecting the Cricut Machine to the Cricut Design Space Apps will be discussed in the next section. You'll also learn to use the Cricut design space interface in the next chapter in detail.

## 2.4: Getting started with Cricut Design Space Software

So now that you've understood what your machine can do and how to get your crafts done efficiently using Cricut, you need to know how to use the device for your good now. The significant part about the machine is the design space interface. The design space app has a lot of advantages to help with your projects, and the best thing here is to learn how to use the software.

Within this section, you will learn to set up your computer, making it as simple as possible not only to go smoothly but also to enjoy your computer without being frustrated. It depends on the technologies that you deal with. It relies on two different contexts. You need to set up a device in one side if you work on a Mac or Windows, then you need to do it on another side while using an Android or an iOS. Most people think this method is complicated, but it's pretty easy, taking ten or fewer steps, which is excellent.

The first way we'll show how your machine can be set up if you operate on an Android or iOS. In this segment, we will go step by step so that the process will go smoothly and without repeating steps. If you try to set up things, it can be very frustrating, so to prevent this, here is a simple guide to doing this.

**Setting up the Cricut design space on your Windows computer**

You will need to follow these guidelines to make your machine work if you are operating on a Windows computer. This configuration is also simple and has fewer steps than mobile device setup instructions.

You will need to follow these guidelines to make your machine work if you are operating on a Windows computer. This configuration is also simple and has fewer steps than mobile device setup instructions.

1. Plug your machine. Don't turn on your machine. Do not trigger or attempt to connect your computer without plugging it in first.
2. Start the computer.
3. Link your computer with the machine. This can be done by two different methods. You can choose what the right choice for you is. Either you can do this with the USB cord, or you can combine it with Bluetooth to connect your phone. Both ways are going to work fine, and it just depends on how you want to do this.
4. Go to the.cricut.com/set-up website in your browser as this is how you complete the installation.
    1. From this stage, you can complete your configuration by ensuring that you carefully follow the guidelines.
5. The on-screen prompts and instructions for signing in and generating your ID must be followed. That would be your future Cricut Tag.
6. Download and install the Design Space software. This will have so many benefits for you later since here you will have access to those benefits.

7. Do not forget that when it tells you to do so, you will need to plug-in.
8. Whenever you want to do your first project, you will be able to see if you did it correctly. Once you get there, your machine is ready to go, and you can do the trial project, and your machine can be used without unnecessarily wasted material.

**Setting up Cricut Design Space on your MAC Device**

the following steps must be taken to connect your Cricut machine for the first time to your MAC.

1. Plug in and power your Cricut machine on.
2. Attach your Cricut to your MAC using the USB cord provided.
3. Opening your web browser is essential, as well as going to www.cricut.com/setup.
4. Log-in to your account at cricut.com.
5. Click "Need a Cricut Account" to set up a new account if you are a new visitor to Cricut.com.
6. You are now eligible to set up your Cricut machine and link it to the design space at Cricut.
7. To start the setup phase, click Continue.
8. Click on the Download tab without wasting too much time.
9. In the MAC toolbar, you'll need to open the finder.
10. Tap on your operating system's download folder and double-click the CRICUTDESIGNSPACE file.
11. Go through the terms and conditions and click on agree.
12. Drag the NPCRICUT. PLUG-IN icon to the plug-in folder of the browser.

13. Click on "Authenticate". This is based on the settings of your device. After beginning on this early step, you will need to enter your administrator name and password.
14. Close the Cricut design space and open windows to return to your browser of choice.
15. In this step, you will have to exit your browser completely, then reopen it and go back to www.cricut.com/setup to continue your setup process.
16. Please check "Detect Machine", upon detection of your machine, click Continue.
17. Check the box to link to your trial and then click on Start.
18. You've set up your Cricut design space and are ready to write, design, or cut your first project.

**Setting up Cricut Design space on your mobile device**

The first step, whether you work with an Android or an iOS, will be to learn how to set up your machine. In this section, you must proceed step by step so that the method will go smoothly and without repeated actions. This can be a frustrating thing when you want to set it up and prevent repetitive steps. So let's start, and then you can get your machine ready.

1. Plug in your machine.
2. Turn on the Power.
3. You'll need to pair your device to your machine (either Android or iOS). To do so, you'll need to use your Bluetooth.
4. Download Space Design Application. You'll need to mount it on your machine too. If you have any concerns about how to use this program, we'll answer it in a later chapter to make it easier for you and the system to realize this app will be able to do so much, so this is a crucial step for you.

5. Click on the menu button
6. Choose the button that says machine setup and application overview
7. Now, select the button that says "new machine setup."
8. The next step is pretty easy because the only thing you need to do is to follow what your screen is saying. On-screen prompts will be provided, which will help you complete the setup.
9. Just make sure the steps have been followed accurately, and that is perfect if you can't go far. Go to the speed at which you are confident and make sure you understand what they want from you. Moving slower can help minimize errors, but you don't feel guilty if you make mistakes. That happens every day to people, and it's easy to fix.

You will know that you've done everything the right way when it tells you that it's time to do your first project, you have done all right and correctly. You know that once this happens, your setup is complete. An additional tip for you is that your computer is already automatically registered during the setup process. If you don't complete the configuration when you connect your computer, you need to reconnect it, and this is something you can't miss because the machine requires to be registered.

# Chapter 3: Working with Cricut Design Space

Working with Cricut design space does not require one to be a master of crafting. You just have to learn a few basic things before you can start using your machine to craft almost anything you can imagine. Working with the device involves setting up the equipment for your project and then configuring the design space application as per your needs. You'll learn these basic yet necessary steps here

## 3.1 : Getting the machine ready

In order to get started on your first project, you first need to get your machine ready for the task. Getting the machine ready requires a few steps, which are mentioned below. Make sure to follow the steps correctly to get your machine ready.

**Loading a pen**

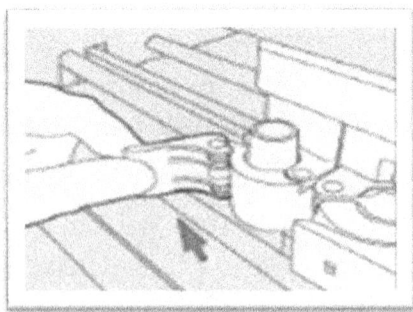

1. To insert the pen, first, open the accessory Clamp A.
2. Smoothly detach the cap from the pen.

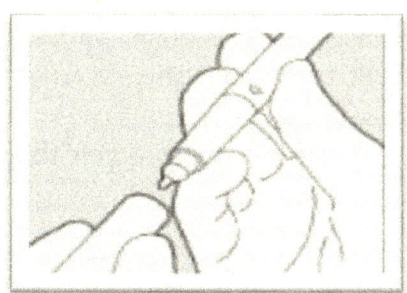

3. Keep clamp A with your fingers while moving the pen down further into the clamp until the arrowhead on the pen disappears.

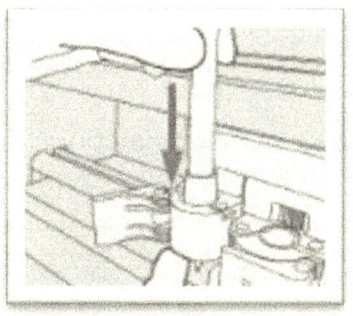

4. Close the hatch gently.

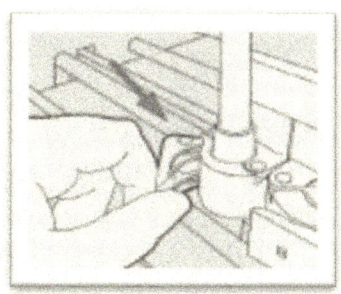

**Preparing and mounting a mat**

5. The next step is to load the black paper provided in your packet of starting materials onto your unique mat. First, you need to remove the protective cover from your mat.
You are cutting, you may need to put this cover aside, but be sure to replace or secure the adhesive of the mat

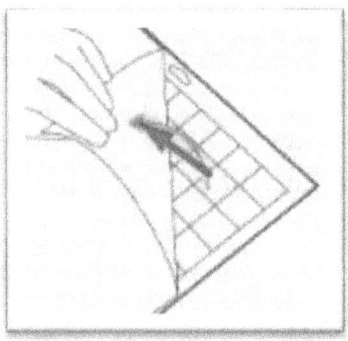

when it is not in use.
6. In the top left corner of your mat, position your paper to the gridlines, and smoothen the paper onto the clean sheet.

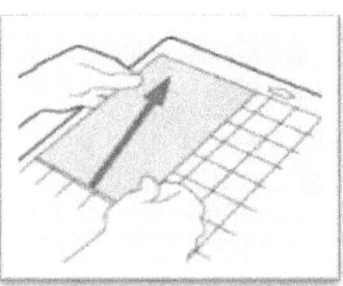

7. Load the mat gently into your Cricut machine by pressing the blinking load / unload button and placing the mat under the mat guides.
When you are at this point, you will undoubtedly know that the mat is loaded when the Cricut logo on the mat is directly under the rollers of the unit.

8. Press the blinking load / unload button to keep the mat tightly pressed against the rollers.

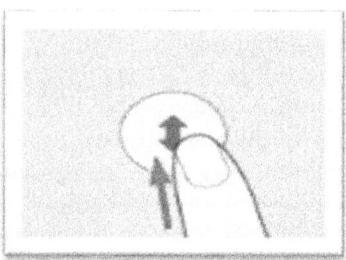

**Remove paper or cardstock from the mat while curling is avoided.**

9. Bend the mat gently till the release of one edge of the material. Make sure that you have removed your pen. Simply open the accessory clamp A and pull the pen straight up. Don't forget to close the pen.

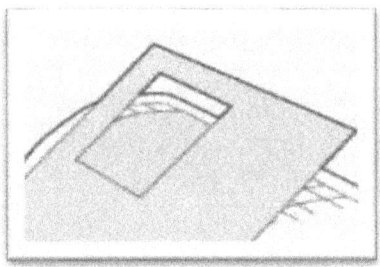

10. Gently remove the card by bending the mat gently until the release of one edge of the card.

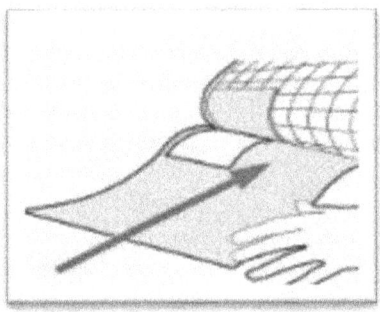

11. You will have to move the mat over to a flat surface at this stage and then pull the mat away from your material gradually until the card releases. A Cricut scraper may be used to remove excess material from the cutting mat quickly

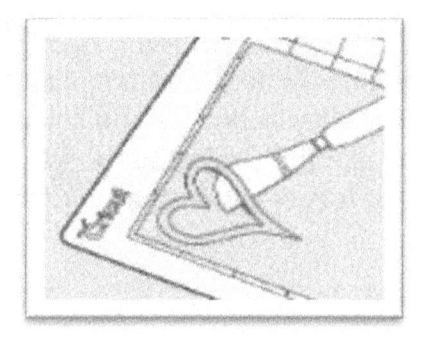

12. Use the scraper to remove residual material fragments.

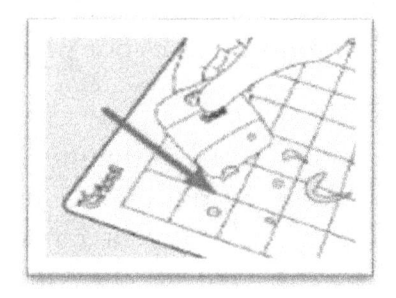

13. Take the jade cards gently from your package of starter materials and fit it into the slots in the card's four corners.

**Choosing vinyl to use with your Cricut Machine:**

Another thing that needs to be sorted out before starting a project with the Cricut machine is the selection of vinyl. As this is the heart of the project and for a project to be successfully crafted, it is essential that you choose a vinyl that matches the best of your interests and provides the best quality.

Various vinyl manufacturers are churning out different craft items, multiple colors, textures, and choices. Pay attention to what piece of vinyl material you are using for your project, so you don't ruin your project. Know the different styles if you have to deal with the vinyl stuff, or use one suggested by the users' community for your project.

**Adhesive vinyl**

This vinyl material is the most popular on the market. You'll come across it frequently with your starter kit in your machine. It comes attached to a silicone-coated carrier sheet so that you can take off the vinyl quickly. Using transmission tape to move it to its final position on your wall, after it has been sliced and weeded.

There are two kinds of adhesive vinyl materials: removable and permanent.

**Removable** adhesive vinyl is the standard Cricut vinyl material often used for indoor, temporary outdoor activities, or put on any surface that does not touch regularly or needs a wash.

**Permanent** vinyl adhesive, on the other hand, is waterproof, and last longer than temporary vinyl adhesive. They're typically expected to last six or more years. It's something that is used in DIY projects involving daily washing such as tumblers, shot glasses, exterior walls, car decals, and more.

### Heat transfer vinyl

This is the form used with the fabrics. It is designed to bind to the fabric when it receives heat and pressure. There is a range of features that can help you decide the best quality of vinyl heat transfer material: color, texture, weeding easiness, size, durability, and efficiency of cutting. Unlike adhesive vinyl, heat transfer vinyl does not require transmission tape.

### Cling vinyl

It is a type of vinyl material that has no adhesive attached to it but uses static electricity to attach to smooth surfaces such as window panels and removable mirror decorations. This can be applied on dry and clean surfaces and reused.

## 3.2: Configuring the Cricut Design Space

The next step required after setting up the machine is to configure the design space as per the requirements of the project. In this section, you'll learn some basic configuration methods that will help you in getting your crafts ready. Working with fonts and images are the most primary operations that are required to create a project in the Cricut Design Space

In this section, you'll learn how to perform different actions concerning working with fonts and images in Cricut Design Space to configure it as per your needs.

### Working with fonts

One of Cricut Design Space's unique features is the ability to highlight the project with unique fonts and text. Many Cricut machine projects start with the Design Space and you know what? There is more to it than just meeting the eye. Let's get started with Design Space fonts.

## Adding text to Cricut Design Space

Navigate to the left side of the canvas for Windows users, and select the Text tool. The Text tool is at the bottom-left of the screen for iOS or Android users.

Pick the font size and type of font you want to use and enter your text in the text box. Before typing the text, don't panic even if you didn't select the font parameters, with Cricut Design Space, you can type the text before choosing the font on Windows / Mac.

To close it press or tap any space outside of the text window.

## Editing Text in Cricut Design Space

It is super easy to edit the text. Double click on the text to view options available. From the list of options provided, pick the operation you wish, including font style, color, size, letter, and line spacing.

## Editing fonts

Pick the text you want to edit on the canvas, or you can insert text from the panel of design or pick a layer of text from the group of layers.

You can start modifying the font using the options available when the Text Edit bar pops up. These options include Text, Orientation, Text Drop-Down, Font Filter, Design, Font Size, Line Space, and more.

## Writing Using Fonts

Changing the line form of your text from 'Cut' to 'Write' is an easy way to compose font using a Cricut pen with a Cricut machine. First, you select the type of font you want to use and choose the "Writing format" of your choosing. Remember that the fonts used in the Writing style are identical to the handwritten text, but the Cricut machine will type it as if it traces the letters outside. This helps you understand how fonts work and how the fonts would look like in the final form.

## System Fonts

System fonts refer to fonts loaded in your mobile device or computer. The Cricut Design Space will automatically access your system fonts any time you sign in and make it possible for you to use them in Design Space projects for free.

Many system fonts have design components that are not compatible with Cricut Design space because Cricut did not design them. Don't be shocked when you experience a failure to import them into the Design Space, or when using them in the Design Space if they behave strangely. When downloading fonts to your tablet or machine, use the instructions on the font site or application.

## Working with images in Cricut Design Space

There are more than 50,000 images in the Cricut library, and these images are updated frequently. The Cricut Design space allows you to use some of these photos for free and find out how they match in with your new project before you purchase them. You can also add your generated images to the canvas.

Here are quick steps on how to use photos in your project:

1. Log in and create a new project in your Design Space.
2. If you are using the iOS / Android app, press the Image button in the bottom left corner of your screen or select Images on the left side of your screen if you are using Windows / Mac computer. Scroll through the photos to pick the ones you want to use in your project.
3. Choose either of the choices below:

- **images** - Use this to search for a particular image in your gallery, or display the photos featured.
- **Categories** - Use this to browse images by choosing the types of images.

- **Cartridges** - Use this to browse or even search for a particular one via the alphabetical list of more than 400 Cricut cartridges.
4. Upload the image(s) you want into your project and start editing it.

## Cutting an image from another image

Using the Slice tool in Design Space, it is possible to remove a part of an image to form another image, and is also relatively simple. Use these steps to extract an image from a separate one:

1. Move the two images to overlap.
2. Pick the two images.
3. Click "Slice" button. This is at the bottom of the Layers Panel for computer users and the bottom of the screen in the Actions menu for Android and iOS owners.
4. Separate the layers for the analysis of your new shapes.
5. Change or delete individual images.
6. Go to the Layer and slice the picture until you get the one you want

## Uploading images to Cricut Design Space

You can upload images you like on to the Cricut design space platform and start your project from there. There are two types of images that you can upload, Basic and Vector images, into the Design Space. Basic images contain file form such as.jpg,.gif,.bmp, and.png, while files such as .svg and .dxf are included in the Vector images.

The step by step instructions on how to upload images to Design Space through various platforms are as follows:

**On Windows / Mac:**

1. Click Upload on the left-hand side of the Canvas interface screen.

2. Using the Browse button to select the image you want from your computer or copy and paste the file to the upload window.
3. Using these steps to upload Basic images:
   - Select your desired simple image file.
   - Open or drag and drop the file to the Layout Space Describe your image as simple, slightly complex or complicated on the screen
   - Select Continue to define your image's cut lines by modifying unwanted background.
4. To show the cut lines in your picture, select the Preview. If the image seems fit to you, choose to Proceed.
5. Name your photo and tag it. Decide also how you plan to store it, either as a Cut or as an illustration of Print and Cut. Note that the entire image will be saved as Print Then Cut.
6. When you have done click Save.
7. If, on the other hand, you intend to upload the Vector image, then use the following steps:
   - Select the Vector image file that you want to upload
   - Open or drag and drop the file to the Layout Space.
   - Title your image, and name it as shown in the Basic choice image.
8. Click the image and pick Photos to be placed on your display screen.

**On iOS Device:**

1. Click the Upload option at the bottom of the toolbar on the iOS device.
2. Use Browse files to check for the image that you want to upload to your device from the available storage applications.
3. If it is the Basic image, clean up the image, and identify the image's cut lines.
4. These methods can be used:
   - **Delete**- this will eliminate linked areas of the same color.

- **Erase** - Use this tool to erase any unwanted areas of the image you wish to drop.
- **Crop**- use this tool to trim your image's edges.
5. After your image has been cleaned, select Next at the top right corner of your screen.
6. Make final changes to your image before saving your collection.
7. Tap Next. Name and save your final picture, either as Cut or Print Then Save.
8. Select the Save option at the top right of your screen.
9. Choose the image from the Uploaded Images Library that will be inserted into the Canvas.

**On Android device**

1. Click the Upload button at the bottom of the panel.
2. Choose to take a picture, select from the photo library, or open uploaded photos.
3. Select the file storage program where your image is stored.
4. To change your image, use the Delete, Erase, and Crop options for Basic images.
5. When the picture has been cleaned, press Finished.
6. Tap Next in the screen's upper right corner.
7. Name your picture and choose how it can be saved.
8. Choose the image you want to add to the Canvas.

## 3.3: Using PDF Files in Cricut Design Space

You can also use PDF files in Cricut Design Space to create your project. Using PDF files in Cricut Design Space does not take a lot of time nor requires any effort. The process is quite simple, and here's how you can do it.

1. Open your Cricut design space attentively and click on

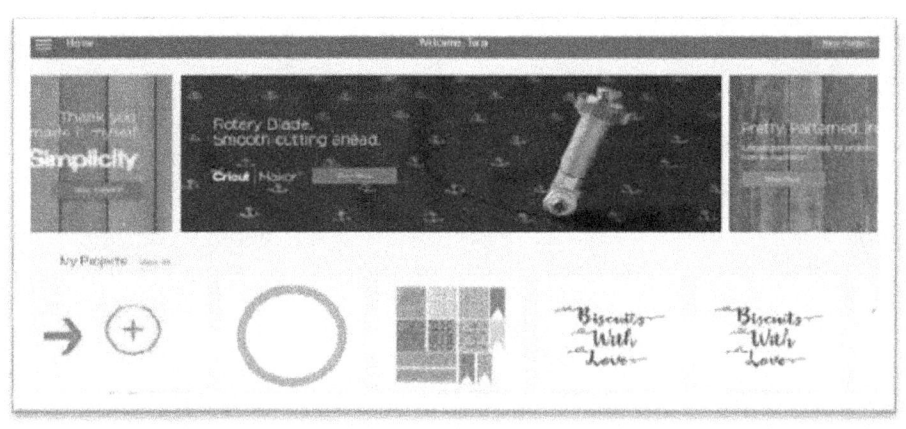

   new project.

2. You need to convert the PDF to a functional file in Cricut Design Space in this phase so you can use a PDF converter conveniently. If you are using a PDF converter, simply

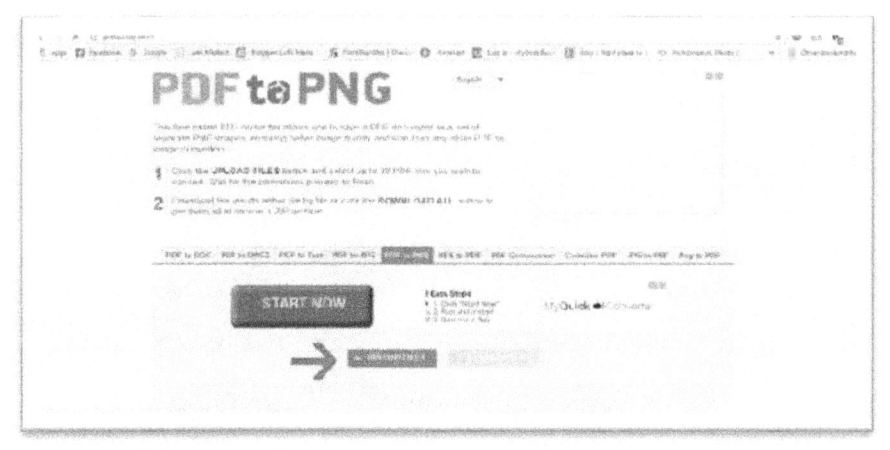

   press Download.

3. A new tab will open up, find, and open your PDF File.

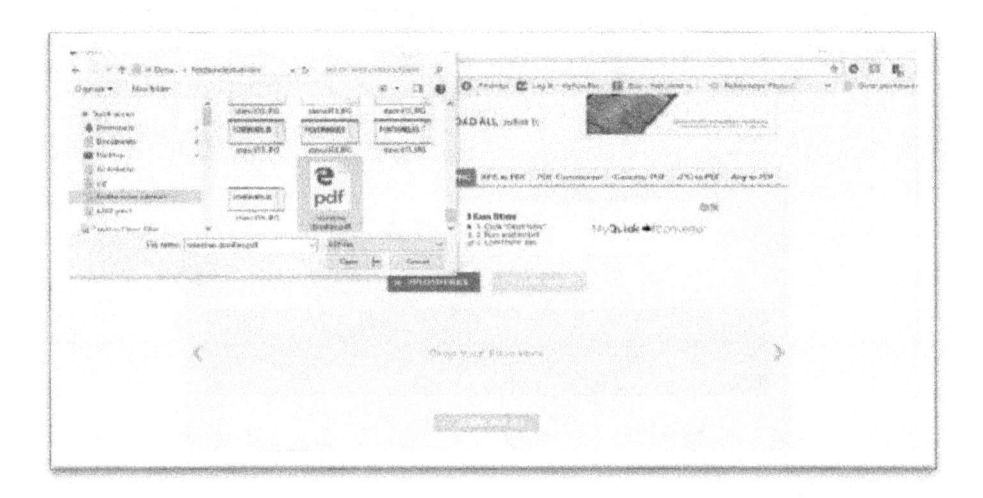

4. Around now, you're about to see your file get converted.

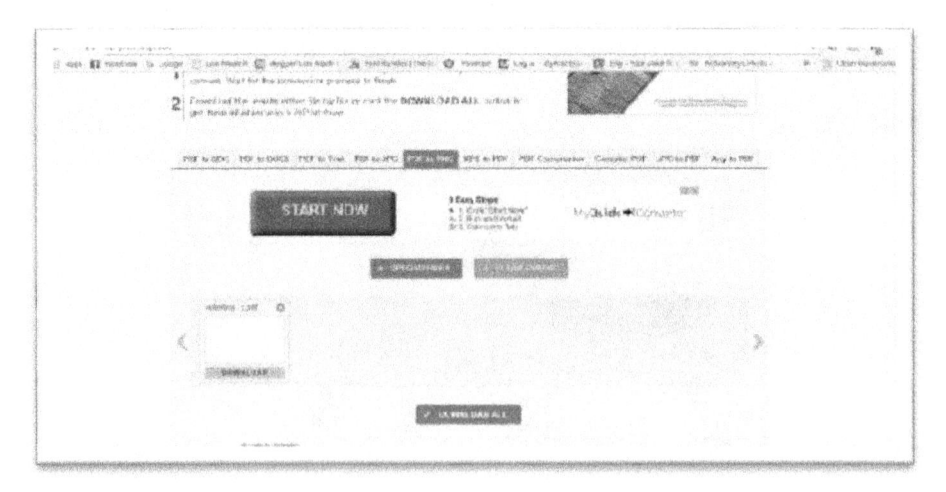

5. Download the new file. It will appear as a zipped file, and after that, unzip the file.

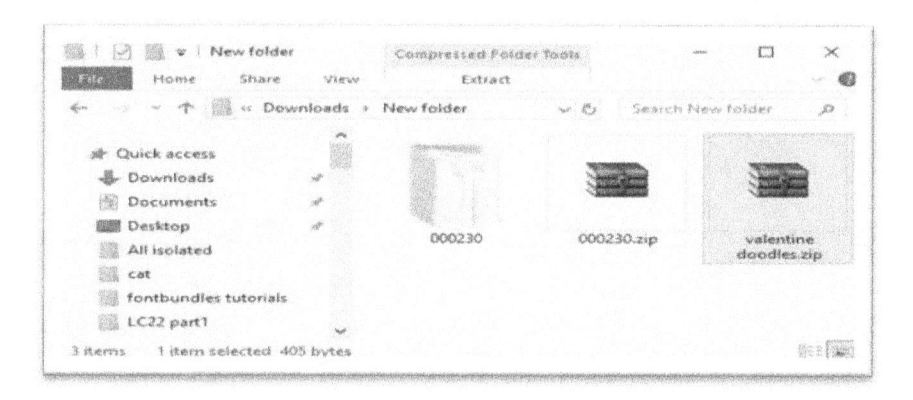

6. You'll need to go back to Cricut Design Space and then

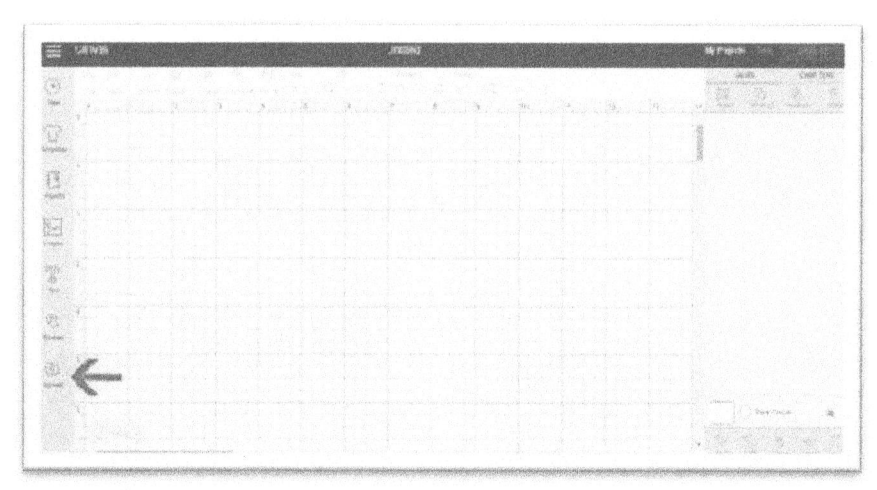

press Upload.

7. Select images to upload.

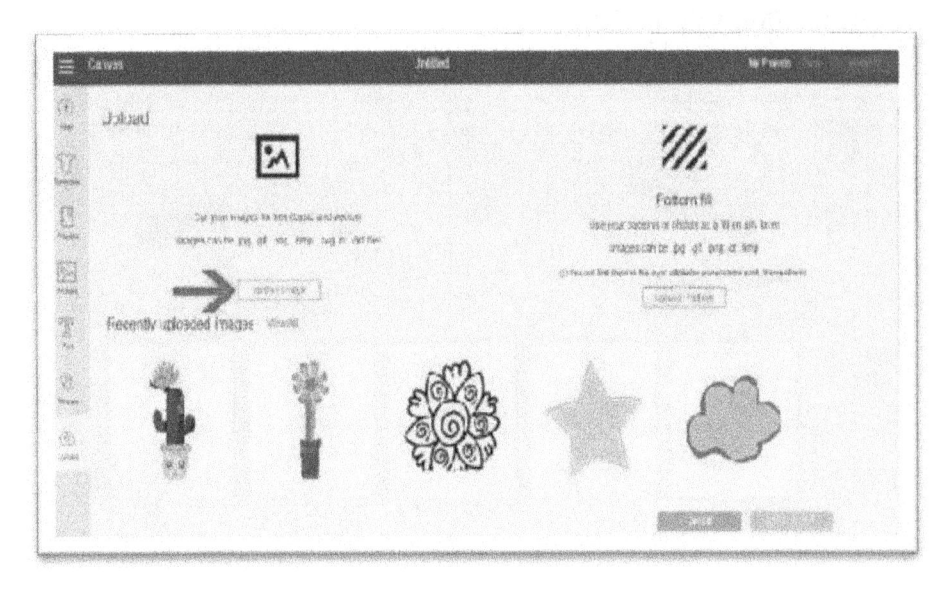

8. Simply press Browse.

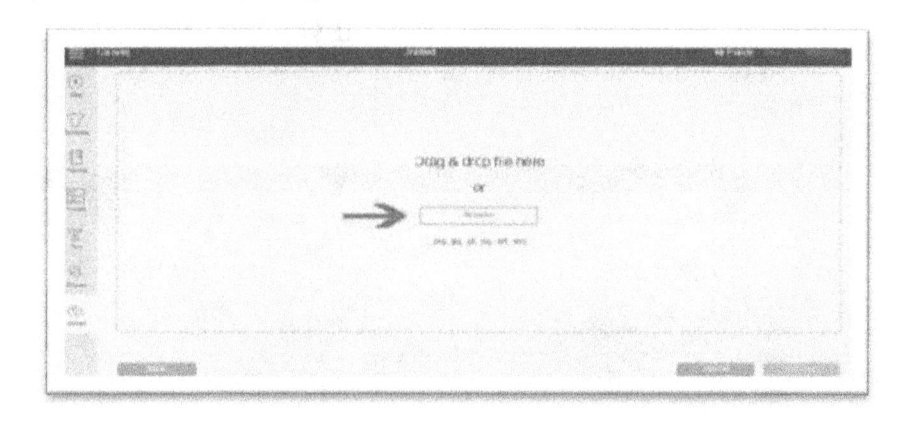

9. Tap on the converted file and select it.

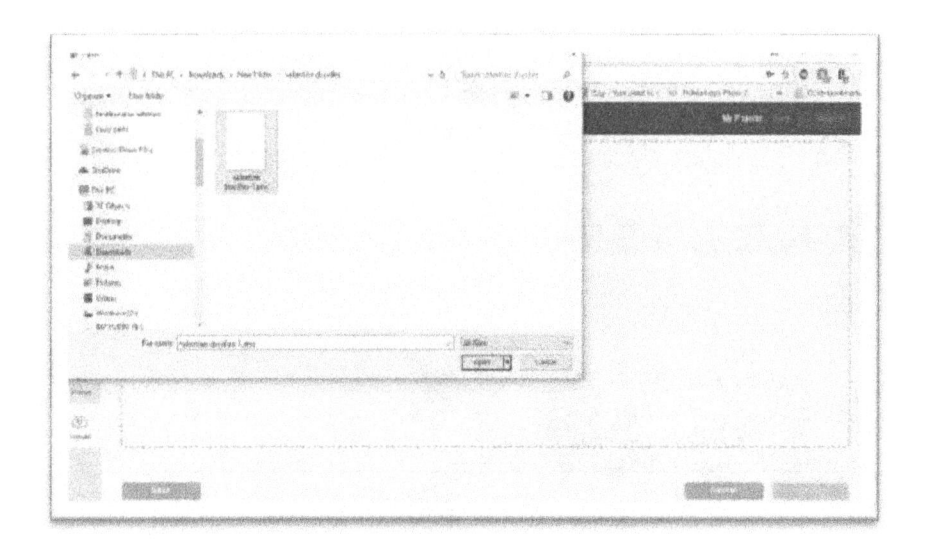

10. The file will appear on your upload picture screen. You can see the white is still around your photos, even though you have converted it to a PNG. If you cut at this stage, all you will have is a full rectangle.

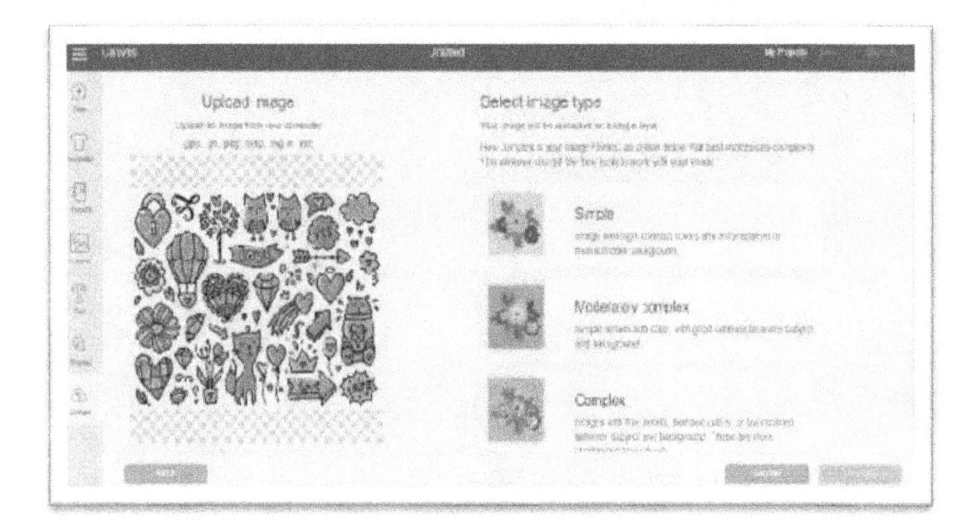

11. You need the white sections to be removed, so you need to press complex and then proceed.

12. Click on the magic wand then click the white area.

13. It will eliminate all the white.

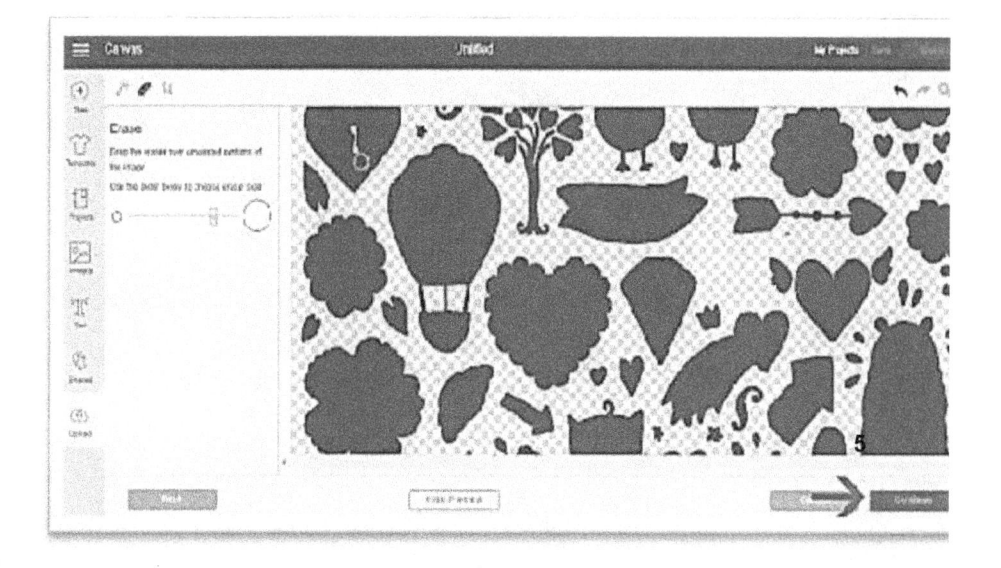

The eraser tool can be used to eliminate any extra bits that you don't need. Click on Preview, once you're satisfied.

14. Test any one of the silhouettes. Each will be A-line cut. Then click Start.

    Select Print and Cut and save.

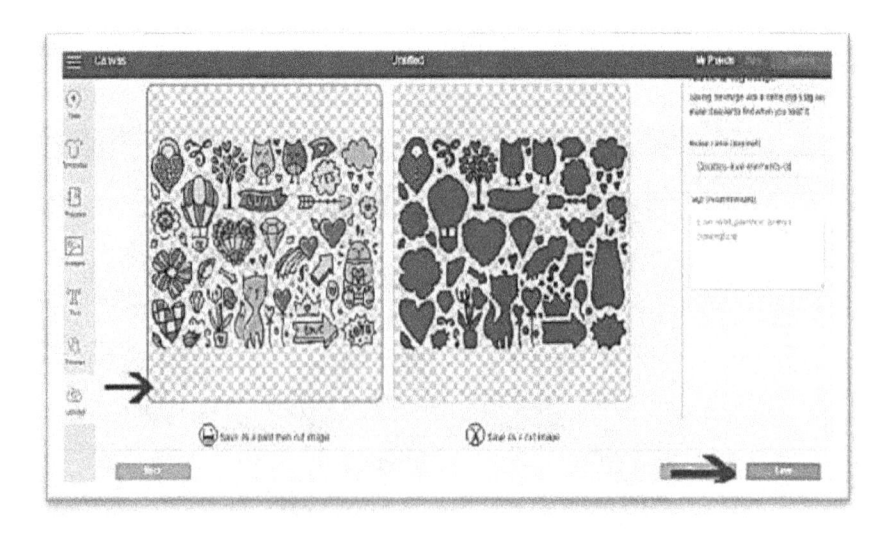

15. . Your file is in your library now. Then choose it and insert

it.

16. Your design should show up in your area of design. Resize and then select make it.

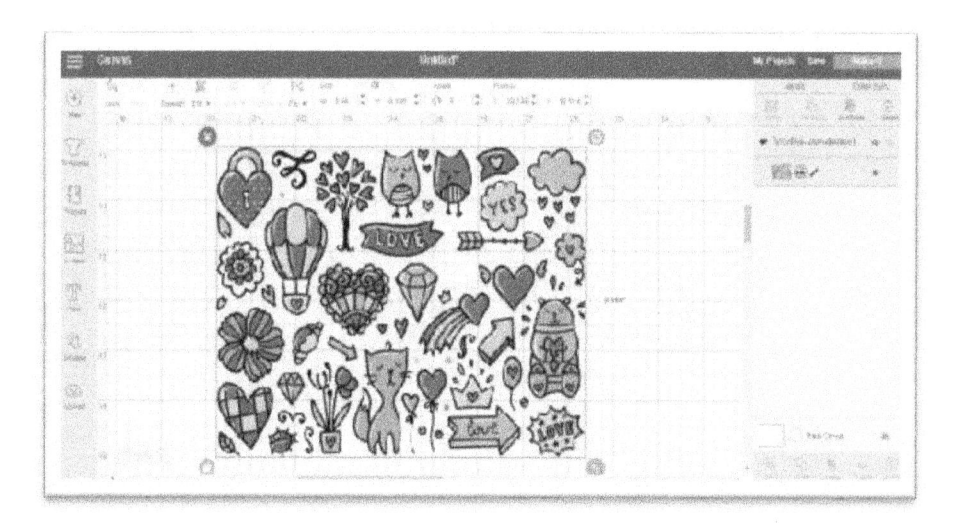

53

17. You can see the print and cut lines across your design, please follow the instructions to print and then cut your design.

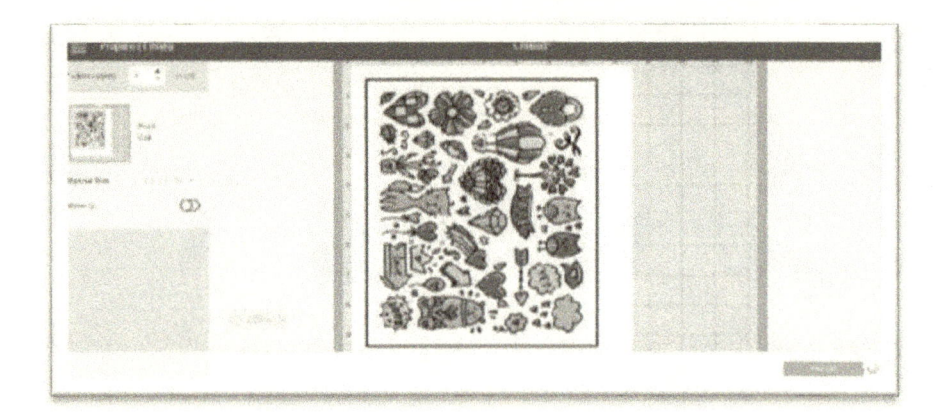

## 3.4: Your first design with the Cricut design space

The first thing you get when you first open the Cricut Design Space is a straightforward tutorial on how to insert a shape and how to fill it with a colored design. Go ahead and go through the phase a few times before you're familiar with where the different assets and choices are, so you can add a shape into the design space, change the Line type, and change what the shape is filled in with. This will provide you a head start in finding out how to do more projects inside the Cricut Design Space!

There's a website that includes a variety of tutorial videos for various things you can do in the design room. Check out videos, troubleshooting, and so much more there. The URL of the website is https:/learn.cricut.com/design-space-for-beginners.

Now that you have got a preliminary feel for some of the fundamentals let's run through a project and familiarize yourself with the whole process.

You'll pick the "Text" option as the first move. Then type the word, "Better Vibes" in the text box that appears, and select a font in the design space you want. Remember some of the fonts in that list are going to cost a lot. Unless you are searching solely for free fonts, you can use the "Service Fonts" which are the fonts already installed on your computer.

After you have selected a font that suits your vision for this project, make sure that the "Line type" is set to "cut." When you've made sure of this, you can click "Make it," in the upper right corner and follow the prompts. If your concept looks good on the pop-up screen, you will be following these next steps.

Cut a piece of vinyl that is suitably designed to match your design using the dimensions at the top of the Design Room. Use your Cricut Maker light blue or medium-grip mat and line up your vinyl so that it's printed on it. Change where your concept is in the Project Room if you need it!

You are using the rounded back of your scraper/furnishing tool to smooth the vinyl down on the grasped sheet, working from the center outwards towards the bottom, until you have your vinyl where you need it. Make sure the piece lies flat with zero bubbles or wrinkles so that you can get the smoothest and accurate cuts possible.

Choose the "vinyl" setting on your Cricut Explore model now that your vinyl is lined up on your mat (skip this move if you have a Cricut Maker). Slide your mat into your Cricut maker under white holding brackets. From there, click on "Continue" in the Cricut Design Space at the bottom right. The platform will connect with your computer, and you will be prompted to press the button with a double arrow. This locks the mat in place.

When you have the Cricut C button blinking, click it once and watch the magic work! Once the machine has finished cutting, remove the mat from the machine and transfer it to your crafting room. Smooth the entire surface of the vinyl on your mat with the rounded back of your scraper/furnishing tool. This will help the sheet of the carrier hang on to the parts of your design you don't want to weed.

Using your weeding tool to pick up the blanks around your letters after you have rubbed the whole piece thoroughly. The history, the O and G circles, all of the stuff you don't want to stick to your laptop. If only the letters are left on the carrier pad, cut a piece of transfer tape of the correct size. Smooth the transfer tape down onto the whole pattern using the back of your scraper. If you have a firm grasp on your template, peel off the tape from the sheet of the carrier.

Clean the space on your laptop using some rubbing alcohol, where you plan to put your design. Once it's clean, use your scraper back to lay the pattern where you want it, and rub it into shape. Carefully peel back your transfer sheet to show off your new template and complement your artistry! You just finished your first project, Cricut! Look at you! You just became an artist whose specialty is to craft.

## 3.5 : Turning your design dreams into reality

Cricut Design Space helps you turn your design dreams into reality and removing any limits from your imagination. And as it's explained what your machine could do, and for what you will use it. Now you need to learn how to make the most of the application. The central part of the software is about the machine. The application has a lot of advantages to help with your projects, and the best thing here is to learn how to use the application.

Open your Cricut Design Space, and you'll see a blue square that says build a new project when you open it and decide to create a new project. When you've done that, you'll find yourself at a place where you can build. This will be empty and white. Clicking on the picture option at the bottom of the screen will take you to a new page.

There is a search option at the upper corner of the screen, and you can type in what you'd like to do. For starters, if you want to make a holiday card, type in the holiday card. Know there are lots of search choices, so try different terms to see new images. The photos on the screen can be different from what you see in other places due to their frequent switching. This company is excellent at regularly improving to give you everything you need, to the point that they offer you fresh ideas in their project center.

Some of them are costly, but most are free. Remember that some are for cutting, and some are for printing. Saying you just have to look for the price at the bottom of the picture is relatively straightforward, or if there is a little printer, then it means it is printable. Note, begin slowly as you get used to the system and how you can work it for you when you just start.

If you think you will be using your computer a lot, then you may consider subscribing to the Cricut Access Standard because it gives you more choices once you have selected your project, press the insert button. At the bottom of the page, you should find this.

Now that you have done this, your project is going to be in the workplace.

When your project is in the workspace, for your first project, you can make any improvements to it that you want. We would recommend making no significant changes because you are not yet used to the app, but as you practice, you can learn more about making various changes and adding your style to your projects.

In this case, it might be minimal for a card, and you might need to make it bigger, and some of them only come with an envelope to make with it, or some need you to do more things to go with it. There are things that you will have to worry about as well. If you want to increase the scale, then you can, of course, make it bigger and enlarge it.

Click on the edit button at the bottom of the screen to do so, and use the width or height section to incorporate the changes you want, and the app will make the changes accordingly. When you have the size you require and are ready to start cutting, click the button "Make it".

At the bottom right of your screen, there will be a green circle. Once you do that, you will be in the area where the cutting mat displays your product. Click the arrow on the right, and scroll to see which cloth you can use or will be using. Going through them is a good idea so that you can get the paper or vinyl ready to be cut in the order as it should be. Then move back to the Start and press Continuing Circle. It'll be a Green Circle.

You can see from here how the first mat is going to be cut so that you can get this ready. Through this, the design space will direct you, so follow the directions once they pop up. Every time you start it, you'll be asked to connect to a nearby computer. That is a natural move, so don't worry about it. The scoring stylus or other materials or objects may be used depending on the project you select, so that is also something to bear in mind. When you use the stylus, make sure it's all the way in, and when it's down, it will press. You'll have to close the latch and have it ready. It is then time to carry out the next step.

You will need to click on the machine's blinking keys. This is to the west. The first is for charging, and the second is for cutting and scoring. Sometimes, you need to match the dial to the material you are using.

Follow the instructions, and it'll tell you when to load and unload. You can then watch the concept breakthrough in the unit. After you have removed it from the mat, you should fold it on the score lines, and it's going to be over. You can use the project in any way you want, but it will also help you get used to spacing as well as saving materials and time starting with something basic.

The app is also ready to do projects, and all you need to do to pick one and be able to use it to your benefit is pick one and go with it. You choose one and give it to your computer and tell it to cut. Once you've built this, in just a few minutes, you'll have a layout that looks professional and glamourous.

Once you see the Cricut Design Space opening screen, you'll know that you're ready to do projects at the bottom, and then by clicking on the word projects, you can click on the list. It is in the bottom left corner. You may limit the quest by category or use the project menu. It is located at the top of the machine along the top toolbar. There are hundreds of items to choose from, and when you have signed in, you can even prefer the designs and find them even better and easier later by clicking on the button that says 'My ready to do projects.' This is going to be on the menu drop-.

One of the items that a lot of people want to do is make personalized type T-shirts. So to do this on the screen, you'd be able to find a ready to create a project you like and then click on the picture. A pop- window will open, and you will get all the information you need. They offer step-- directions that can be printed and held alongside you if appropriate. There will be two different buttons that pop up down along the edges.

You may and do customize it. If you want to do so, in your design room, you automatically will be forwarded to the cut screen. All of the design elements will be designed and colored precisely, as shown in the picture, and all you need to do is start.

Nevertheless, before you start cutting the design, it's essential to know that you can't change the color, scale, or any other aspect of the model at this point (once you're on the cut screen) if you don't like how it looks in the photo you need to repair it first.

When you are dealing with iron-on products, you must also press the mirror button on will cut mat because it does not automatically see them and do it for you. If you pick the premade custom design, it will be loaded onto the canvas of the design space we spoke about above. You can also edit every aspect of the design while you're here just as you can select your projects, and hence the premade layouts can be a perfect jump-off point for your creative creations. If you're happy with the configuration edits, hit the green make it button to submit out the cut template. Growing project ready requires guidance on how to cut different materials for each particular project. You need to follow the prompts that show up on the computer from there.

If you have the computer for the canvas, this applies to the computer on which you will be designing. Click the new Project button as such. Then, the canvas will open up. Now we can get your project underway. There's also zoom in and out button for you to see the info on your bottom left corner, which are a little harder to see. You can find the key buttons on the left side of your screen, which are for you to use.

- The new button will launch you with a new project.
- The Template button is one element that will help you work on various things in your project. Here you can change the template scale, as well as the color.
- The different projects will be released in the CDS.
- Photos are where the images you can purchase from the app can be found, but also the images you uploaded.
- Shapes will show you forms and score line. By combining various types, you can create a multitude of different designs.
- The text displays the text on the drop-down menu and helps you find the font you want.
- Upload is how you transfer to your device the png, jpeg, or SVG file you have saved too.
- 

Buying one thing at a time is a good idea because it will save you from being distracted at the outset.

You do have filters on the CDS, so that's a huge time saver. You can use your filters to narrow down the things you submitted, or the items in the Access app.

Recently the preview screen has been revamped to look better, and now you can even switch stuff around before cutting it on this screen.

The app should try to save you as much material as possible. Still, sometimes you've cut with huge gaps between the cuts, and the opportunity to be able to step into those spaces manually over other cuts is a charming tip the preview screen provides. You do have a lot of editing tools in this app, and when you want to use them, it is pretty straightforward. All you have to do is look at the cornerstone of the screen, and when you make your designs, that will help. She will be in the top right corner. And that'll be able to see things and how they can function.

In this app's bottom right corner, you'll see a few more choices for you. You will see slice first. Slice means you can cut pictures or slice objects from others. It'll even let you make monograms of split letters.

You can see flat, which means you can flatten your picture together so you can print it out.

Contour, which means you erase the pictures or unnecessary lines inside or outside. It is so that the photos have become the way you want them to be.

Attach means that you add text or pictures in such a way that they are cut out precisely as you have them on the canvas. The next Catch. It sticks to cursive names. And it's a straight line with no stories to pick. The wheeled objects transform themselves into one entity.

The upper right corner of the device also features a stand. Open, and you'll panel the layers and sync the light. The sync color will let you see how many colors you have, and how many canvases you have. By dragging and dropping items in this panel, you can shift objects to the same color. The panel of layers will allow you to see all the different layers of your photos, and you can click on the eyeball to unhide or mask some levels.

Since most people use fonts in their Cricut machine and want to make different T-shirts or designs, they will need to know how to use and get the typefaces. If you make custom designs, it is effortless to add the fonts to the Cricut space once you learn how to do it. For the best fonts you can find for free, there are several different web pages.

Google fonts are one of the leading examples of this. Both are open-source and free fonts. The one is called Dafont. It also has plenty of free fonts for personal use, so click download when you go to the web, and you find a font that you like all you need to do. And save the file to your Mac. Setting up a folder for the fonts is a lot simpler. It is particularly true with all of your fonts because if you do not organize, it will be tough to keep track of them once you start collecting them. The font must be downloaded and is more than likely a zip file.

To get this to work perfectly, all you have to do is right-click the file and then press Extract all. Typically, if you like, you can uninstall the original record, so it doesn't clutter your data on your desktop. If you have another tab, you need to find the file on your computer and open the exact type file where all of your fonts are. To open it, you'll need to double-click the file.

This will open into your font screen. Depending on where and how you get your fonts from, you can obtain only an exact type of file and no other choices, which are good because your computer can still work with it. You will need to press the Update button from here.

You will find this at the top of the window that has just opened on your screen, and then load the font on your screen. Now that your machine has the font loaded, which is all you have to do. You'll be able to scan for and locate your design room the next time you open it up. You may or may not show up when you go into the design space and find your font after building a text box.

When it doesn't turn up correctly, then you'll have to find out why. When you find you're the font, try refreshing the page correctly, and if that doesn't work, sign in and then sign back out of the app and check to see if that will do the job. If any of these do not work, you will need to restart your computer because this will certainly address any font issues in the system.

Within the interface space, even you can customize your fonts. You may change the font size or style, and also decrease or increase the space between the letters. Another thing you can do is attach your tags to each message so that you can manually switch each letter to exactly how you want it. It makes your projects unique and makes your ideas stand out because you can play so much with them. You can use several different ways to make the letter smaller or more significant, and you can make it artistic with your face or more. The choices are infinite, and you have so many things you can do to change the font to exactly how you want it to be, and that is perfect for people to use because it makes it feel like your own.

You can also find particular fonts you need by filtering them by single layer cutting, multi-layer cutting, or writing. Here is a perfect find for discovering fonts with an ability to write fonts and fonts that have a choice to write. You may also alter how the text style appears on the edit pad, and how the text style to write is.

You can also change the text to write in the edit panel for fonts that have the write option, and then you can see what your text would look like when it is written. Make sure you group or add your letters in such a way that the text is written the same way on the canvas, or the letters will be mixed. So now that you've been able to understand how to connect the files to your office, and do what you need to learn about it. This is very simple, and once you have followed how to do it, it's elementary. Here we gave you all the information you need to create amazing fonts on your Cricut machine and use it for your benefit.

The app they sell to you mainly is superior technology. There are a few features that many people would like to see added. Still, they are continually upgrading to try to satisfy customers' demanding needs to customers' not so demanding needs. But overall, it works well, and it's a massive help for people. The most significant thing people have found is that loading can take a while, it can crash or freeze, and often it just doesn't open at all.

And we will tell you how you can fix those problems. The biggest issue with this app is that you may have reduced access to the Internet. The software needs robust and reliable speeds for Upload and download and a stable connection. If you have an irregular spikes link and dips, this may cause the program to function correctly. If your computer is closer to your modem, you'll likely get a more stable link in this situation.

Sites such as YouTube are a perfect example of this. YouTube still needs a pretty high transfer speed, but with the slower upload speed, you can get away and still get it running. And it's different from the web. This software needs both a good upload speed and a good download speed so that you are continuously sending and receiving information while you work on each application.

So now that you've covered the basics of Cricut Design Space and all its primary operations, the next chapters will be about the materials you can use with your machines and the capabilities of your Cricut machines.

# Chapter 4: Materials & Accessories for working with Cricut

A Cricut machine is considered by many to be just for cutting paper or vinyl, but it can do so much more than that. There are many materials which can be cut by the Cricut machines. Here in this chapter, you will be provided a complete guide to the stuff that your machine can cut, the absolute wonders it can do, and the supplies and accessories that any beginner of Cricut requires to start with this machine to do incredible crafts.

## 4.1 : Which materials the Cricut machines can cut?

Like you have probably read in this book already, Cricut boasts being able to work with over 100 materials to bring your designs to life like never before. Thanks to the broad array of media that Cricut can carry to your crafting station, the possibilities are endless for what you can do with your Cricut machine, regardless of which model you use for your projects.

Cricut machines can cut so many materials that your imagination is the only limit. If you're thinking of what you can use with your Cricut machine, you'll be amazed to know what these machines are capable of. These incredible machines can do everything from cutting anything as fragile as tissue paper to something as thick and heavy as leather.

**Paper and Cardstock:**

The Cricut machine is perfect when it comes to cutting paper and cardstock, but it's not just cutting scrapbook paper.

Check out all the different paper varieties that a Cricut machine can cut:

Adhesive Cardstock, Copy Paper, Construction paper, Cereal box, Cardstock, Flat cardboard, Flocked cardstock, flocked paper, Foil embossed paper, foil poster board, freezer paper, glitter cardstock, glitter paper, craft board, craft paper, Metallic cardstock, metallic paper, metallic poster board, notebook paper, paper grocery bags, parchment paper, paper board, pearl cardstock, pearl paper, photographs, photo framing mat, post its, poster board, rice paper, scrapbook paper, shimmer paper, solid core cardstock, watercolor paper, wax paper, and white core cardstock.

**Vinyl:**

Vinyl is another fantastic material that can be cut by the Cricut machine. Vinyl is perfect to render tags, decals, styles, and graphics.

The types of vinyl that a Cricut machine can trim are:

Adhesive vinyl, Chalkboard vinyl, dry erase vinyl, glitter vinyl, glossy vinyl, holographic vinyl, matte vinyl, metallic vinyl, outdoor vinyl, printable vinyl, stencil vinyl, iron-on vinyl, flocked iron-on vinyl, foil iron-on vinyl, glitter iron-on vinyl, holographic iron-on vinyl, matte iron-on vinyl, metallic iron-on vinyl, neon iron-on vinyl, and printable iron-on vinyl.

**Fabric and textiles:**

The Cricut machines do a great job at all in cutting fabrics, but before cutting, you certainly need to add a stabilizer like Wonder Under or Heat's Bond. Certain fabrics and textiles can be cut without any difficulty with Cricut machines and turned into pieces of art. The fabrics with which the Cricut machine can do wonders are mentioned as:

Burlap, Canvas, Cotton fabric, Denim, Duck Cloth, Faux Leather, Faux Suede, Felt, Flannel, Leather, Linen, Metallic leather, Oilcloth, Polyester, Printable fabric, Silk and Wool felt.

**Other materials:**

There are plenty of other specialty materials besides fabric, paper, and vinyl that a Cricut can cut as well. Here's a list of some:

Adhesive Foil, adhesive wood, aluminum sheets, aluminum foil, balsa wood, birch wood, cork board, corrugated paper, craft foam, duct tape, emboss able Foil, foil acetate, glitter foam, magnet sheets, metallic vellum, paint chips, plastic packaging, printable magnet sheets, printable sticker paper, shrink plastic, soda can, stencil material, tissue paper, temporary tattoo paper, transparency film, vellum, washi sheets, washi tape, window cling wood veneer, and wrapping paper.

You can cut more stuff if you have the Cricut maker. The Cricut maker has the 10 times cutting power of the explorer machines, plus it has a rotary blade and a knife blade to cut even more objects. The Cricut maker can cut materials up to 2,4 mm, plus more than 125 + fabric styles, including:

Chiffon, cashmere, fleece, jersey, jute, knits, moleskin, muslin, seersucker, terry cloth, tulle, tweed, and velvet.

## 4.2 : What the Cricut machines can craft?

There is no restriction to how much your Cricut machine can do. You just have to think of an idea, and the Cricut machine will give the desired shape to it. If you're short on ideas, though, here are some you can use to get your creative juices flowing. Browse through this list and come up with some stuff you think will match well with the types of designs you want to make.

- Make felt dolls
- Beautifully address envelopes
- Create doll clothing

- Make greeting cards of every design and style
- Create placards
- Cut items out of balsa wood
- Cut washi tape shapes
- Craft borders and decorations for your corkboard
- Dream up refrigerator magnets
- Customize wedding invitations
- Create holiday crafts
- Design or decorate purses and wallets
- Cut your craft foam shapes
- Create decals and patterns for pillows and cushions
- Create your coloring book pages
- Cut fabric with precision
- Make jewelry
- Make party favors
- Create 3D bouquets
- Cut leather
- Cut your party hats
- Make themed window clings
- Create fabric appliques
- Create temporary tattoos
- Create glassware decals
- Design personalized gift tags
- Create clothes for your pet
- Create custom gift boxes
- Customize baby clothes

- Design creative pincushions
- Create cake toppers
- Customize holiday ornaments
- Custom Coasters
- Create sewing patterns
- Create themed t-shirt transfers
- Make personalized fabric key fobs
- Cut perfect quilting squares
- Create and embellish your holiday stockings
- Craft decorations to fit any theme
- Design dust covers
- Cut unique stencils
- Create stickers & decals
- Design Door Hangers
- Create jigsaw puzzles
- Add pizzazz to headbands
- Create fabric accessories and embellishments
- Cut patterns to make your socks and embellishments
- Create wedding place cards
- Make 3D paper craft shapes
- Write beautiful signs in calligraphy
- Create cupcake flags
- Craft cushion transfers
- Design 3D and flat-panel wall art of any theme
- Cut scrapbook embellishments
- Cut fun shapes and scrapbooking letters.

- Make personalized gifts, handmade, for any special occasion.
- Design a t-shirt.
- Create a necklace crafted from leather.
- Create buntings and gifts for other events.
- Create your paint stencils.
- Paint a vinyl sticker for the windshield of your car.
- Label things in the pantry, or a game room.
- Design pillows with monograms.
- Make your own Christmas decorations.
- Decorate a tumbler, pan, or cup. Engrave glass at home.
- Build a decal on your wall.
- Paint a wooden sign with color.
- Make clings for your window.
- Design squares of the quilt.
- Design a stand mixer with decals.

## 4.3: Essentials for working with Cricut

When you start working on Cricut projects, you will need some essentials to get going. There are a lot of instruments and accessories that go with these devices, and they will all bring benefits to your projects and make your life easier. Within this section, we'll go through the various tools and accessories that can be used with these machines, as well as a summary to help you see why you would benefit from them.

Here's an overview of what these essentials are:

**Your Cricut Machine:**

Once you've selected the model that's right for you from those described in the first chapter, you'll want it to be set up, equipped, and ready, with the fine point blade loaded into the attachment clamp B.

**Cricut Machine Cutting Mat:**

This mat is a very basic but essential part of the Cricut's process of crafting. Cricut has many thin pads, with an adhesive grip and a pattern on them. When your material is poured onto this mat and loaded into your Cricut machine, you can be confident that your material is right where it needs to be, to get the perfect cuts and strokes on it. This is one of the materials best left to the Cricut brand, due to its unique size and grip strength. Looking for another mat with equivalent skills may end up being much more expensive, or just less effective. Cricut brand is really the one for this particular component.

**Your Hand Tools:**

With things you have around the house, you can fulfill some of the purposes covered by the tools in this list. Cricut does sell a starter kit that includes all of these devices. Nevertheless, this kit is very reasonably priced and contains everything you may need to get started.

**A Blank Stage for Your Design:**

This is the object you'll mark your concept on. It is essential to know that while the world is your oyster and with Cricut crafting, there is very little that is unavailable to you, experts suggest a flat surface for your first project. Being able to view the entire surface of this object, without having to worry about curvature or other obstructions, will make learning how to work with your materials much more uncomplicated.

Although a travel mug is an excellent idea for a Cricut project, doing it as your first one may give you more trouble than you may have expected at first. You don't want to embark on a project that will cause you trouble. Consider then placing a custom template or expression on your screen, or a binder.

## A Computer with Internet Access:

The Cricut Design Space can only be reached through an active internet connection, so it is vital to ensure that your computer has consistent internet access during your design! You may also want to save your job, just in case the link hiccups. In such a scenario, you wouldn't want to risk any design development.

## Transfer Tape:

Transfer tape is a transparent, mild to moderate adhesive tape that is inserted into sheets. The purpose of this material is to take from their back sheet your freshly cut designs, hold them firmly in place correctly, which you can then quickly burnish onto your project. The adhesive is such that it will not damage your design or the material it is intended to continue with.

While transferring tape is an absolute necessity when doing projects with your Cricut machine, the brand doesn't matter for as much as having something to use.

Like any new craft, you are undergoing, finding the supplies and products that best suit your needs, and which will work best for you in the long run, will wake up a bit of trial and error.

## Isopropyl or Rubbing Alcohol:

Since the adhesive is a significant theme and part of the Cricut process and the process of using your Cricut machine, it is vital to make sure that the surfaces you use (your mat, the materials, the item on which your design is to be burnished) are cleaned as best as possible.

You'll want to rub the surface with some rubbing alcohol, especially with a slick surface like glass or ceramic, to remove any dirt, oil, debris, or anything that might compromise your design. If you wipe it with alcohol rubbing, pat dry, then let it stand for thirty seconds, and your design is ready.

**The vital accessories:**

Some numerous tools and accessories can all add value to your projects and make things easier. We will be going through various instruments and accessories in this chapter to help you to see how you can take advantage of these machines.

**Blades:**

The most important thing to talk about is the blades because you can choose from many different options. The Cricut has many different blades, all of which serve a particular purpose for your machine, and it may be confusing to know which one to use. In this section, we will explain the differences in the following blades:

**The excellent point blade** is a machine workhorse. You can use it for almost everything you'll have to do with a new Cricut machine. The blades are covered in white rubber that is new when taken from the company itself. There are a lot of other cheaper options available. However, the places to purchase them cheaper may not work as well, so you will have to research them thoroughly. The blades have a 45-degree angle and are used in both the machine series.

**Bonded fabric blade** has a rosy case and can also be used on both sets. But with the Maker, the rotary wheel works much better. This blade is used to cut material that is attached to fusible support. However, the rotary wheel does not require support.

**The rotary wheel** comes with the Maker and cuts the fabric while being extremely sharp. If you cut a lot of fabric and have a kit to change the blade, the blade must be replaced quite often. Some of the makers won't come with this blade when you buy them, but again you can't purchase it anywhere else, so you have to call the company Cricut, and they'll send it to you for free. You also need a material mat to avoid your material raveling when you cut fabric, as it happens many times or can occur many times.

**The deep point blade** has a black container with a black cover, and you buy it from Cricut too. You can also buy from cheaper spots. The blade is only used on thicker or more robust materials such as foam or magnets and has a sixty-degree steep angle. This can also be found for both series.

The next blades we will discuss are perforation, wavy debossing, and the engraving blades. These four blades are new, and many people haven't got them yet. You can find them in full housing or a quick change tip.

**The wavy blade** can cut a wavy line across your projects like the scissors that came out about a decade ago to cut wavy lines into paper and were such a hit among instructors and paper crafters. It is excellent for cutting screws for tear-problems, and the debossing blade works a bit deeper like a scoring tool on an Explorer machine. The graved blade will only be engraved in metal and other materials, but an important note is created. It is a good idea to keep checking, because even if we have a master list in this section, the company changes it periodically and it is good to stay on updated. It's a great way to keep your material checked, too.

**The scoring wheel** is only for the Maker, and it's the same as the scoring stylus for the Explore machines, but there are a few variations. The blade is very smooth, and can also be fitted with a double marking blade. The scoring blades are the first to have a rapidly changing housing, and the bottom pops off, and a new type of blade can be attached. You can buy the tip for the new blades that are a little cheaper than buying the complete system if you have fast change housing.

**The knife blade** is like a knife which cuts leather, the wood of balsa, among many others. It's for the Maker only, and when you use the app, you must calibrate it because it will have to remind you about it if you don't use it. You can also adjust the cutting pressure, but the warning goes hand in hand. There's no start to try this, and it certainly isn't the first thing you're supposed to try. If you have a problem cutting the material, don't change the settings first and try another way to correct the problem.

Cricut does not guarantee that it will cut a material, which is why you should always search for their website for updates or adjustments. Additionally, the material pressure can be changed, but not more than one or two at a time. Another warning is to be very careful with the knives, so assure you are as careful as you can so that you don't hurt yourself.

Cricut also gives the following instruments, and one of the things you would want to purchase is a weeder instrument. Some of the most effective instruments you can use is a weeder- since the spatula and the pioneering machines can be useful. If you are trying to remove the vinyl from your mat, the weeding tool is necessary. There are many tools for weeding, so everyone works to securely raise vinyl from their back sheet to prevent damaging the project and to keep their mat ruined.

Nonetheless, you can use the weeder tool or buy the weeder toolset if you want an instrument that is direct from the company itself because it has finer points and will do more for you.

Some of the other standard weeding tools are dental picks, but you can use an Exacto knife, but you should be careful not to harm the project or hurt yourself. Even they use an old gift card or a credit card, but you need to be mindful that the product may be scratched, so you must take great care.

**The Spatula:** This is the next device you should learn about. The spatula raises material out of the cuts when the material is not to be torn. The spatula is responsible for this by quickly extracting the substance from the mat. It can also be used in a scraper device to keep the mat clean and clear of debris. At a very reasonable price, Cricut even markets the scraper and spatula together.

**The Scrapper:** Let's talk about the scraper tool now since we have talked about the spatula. For a successful project, a clean mat is essential to ensure that the material doesn't move during cutting. When you are investing a significant amount of money, the last thing you want is that you have to move halfway through the project and then start from the very beginning. Specific tools solve the problem, but the scraper is much quicker, and you have a beautiful clean mat. There are different sizes, but most people choose the extra-big one because it can be easier to carry, and this is easier than the smaller one.

**The Mats:** Extra mats are also preferable, so you don't have to realize that your mat is no longer smooth when working on a project. There are specific ways to put your mat, and you can save your money, but as it's always a good idea to have a few more available if you want. In various tasks, the mats do specific things such as the following:

- The pink used for the fabrics is just for fabric, of course.
- With more substantial projects like canvas, poster board, or heavier card paper, a firm grip, which is the purple one, will be safer.
- For iron-on and vinyl, a green mat is typical.
- For paper and card inventories programs, the light blue will be excellent.

They also offer a toolkit that contains nearly every item we talk about. The toolkit contains the following products:

- Tweezers
- Weeder

- Spatula
- Scraper
- Scissors
- Scoring stylus

You will cut back on much money by buying this instead of purchasing the items individually if you purchase the package instead.

**Bright pad:** With several different reasons, a bright pad is perfect because it makes weeding so much simpler and it makes the cut lines far more noticeable, so if you have something more than a basic cut, it can also help you out because you can see exactly where the lines are. You might also use it to adjust patterns and trace them.

**Heat Press:** A simple press is also excellent. When you are still using the iron for heat transfer vinyl, the easy press makes it so much more straightforward than iron because after one or two wares, there is no peeling, and it also takes out all the speculation about the correct time and temperature. If you have room, you can get a real heat press for just a little bit more financially if you can afford it, but first, considering a beginner heat press mainly if you are doing it in a large quantity or for commercial purposes would be better.

**Brayer Device:** For larger vinyl projects or working with cloth, a brayer device is exceptional. This solves the issue of not having the material completely stabilized before cutting. A brayer does adhere the material to the surface, however, without damaging it.

**Paper trimmer:** If you want to get a straight cut, a paper trimmer is super handy. You don't have to use scissors and do not need a ruler. As such, it makes it much easier for you to cut mainly if you are working with vinyl.

The company also offers its own trimmer, but there are other places where you can still buy a trimmer, and if you go for a simple paper trimmer, you have the option to try and get a perfect fold so you may want to look into it.

**Scissors:** Scissors also make a significant difference. The company scissors are made of stainless steel, which, while remaining durable, creates even cuts as stainless steel is one of the most durable materials available. The scissors are very sharp and come with a micro-tip blade, which means that it is simpler and safer to operate on the fine details in a smaller area right down to the point. It also has an adjustable colored cap, which is also secure, so your scissors can be safely placed.

**Tweezers:** The tweezers are super helpful, and there's more than one form available for people. They usually have one for little things, and the other for vinyl. This tool is in the Cricut toolset, but there are Pazzlee needle point tweezers if you want to go for something else, and these tweezers have a sharp point, which makes it excellent for vinyl. The points are also sharp enough to be able to select delicate bits from the mat without using the edges or some other little trick and they can also pick up the tiniest little scraps. When you don't want to use the company's tweezers, you can probably go for this other provider instead.

**Pens**: These are also a significant part of the Cricut world, and you can buy those pens in a variety of locations. Yet you can also use other pens that you can find just about anywhere, and also for meager prices. More detail about the pens that you can use can be found on the Cricut user's community platform on the internet.

The other tools you can get for yourself are if you find you are a busy person and you go to the houses of other people, or you go on business trips or things of that nature, then you may need a tote bag to hold all your Cricut supplies and machines. The company is selling a nice tote at a fair price you'd be able to use for your gain, and then you'll be able to keep things organized and smooth as it should be. If you don't like their price point, there are also a lot of other places you can also get a decent bag.

You can also get rotary blades or a knife for power. A control knife that's necessarily like an Exacto knife, but you'll have to be careful about it, because even though it brings consistency and consistency to your ventures, you could end up cutting yourself pretty severely, so you'll have to be careful.

If you need rulers because you feel you aren't precise enough, they do have all of these, and they have the different models as well as packs that have all the equipment you need, and you don't need to purchase anything individually. It is a wonderful thing to look at, so that you can see what you like. There are several different websites on the internet where you can find machine tools and each one boasts that their materials are better than the others. Cricut sells everything you'd like on their site, and they provide very fair rates, but if you find their stuff isn't what you'd want, and you'd like anything else, you can do some additional searching too. If you plan to buy these additional devices, you will find that your tasks will go much faster, and you will also be able to get more accuracy and precision with them. For just that reason, many people who like the Cricut and their company are recommending having those pieces.

**Software:**

'**Sure cut A lot** 'is a program from a third party that allows you to cut any shape you can imagine effortlessly immediately. It can easily be used with most electronic cutting devices, including Cricut Explore / Maker, CraftRobo / Graphtec, Vinyl Express, and more. Use 'Sure Cuts A Lot' to design your shape and export it to your Design Space Cricut machine using a licensed format in order to work with your

Cricut Explore machine. It's an excellent craftsmanship app. You won't regret giving it a try.

Keep in mind that this app needs a firmware update to your Cricut Explore machine, incorporates freestyle drawing tools, auto-trace capabilities, and over 200 built-in shapes.

Now that you've learned about all the essentials that are very much required to begin your first project. You're all set. Now you'll be getting some creative ideas in the next chapter to use your Cricut design space to create amazing crafts.

# Chapter 5: Creative Cricut project ideas

After getting the machine, the first thing you need to do is to make some fantastic crafting, and you then start to think of ideas for your projects to do with your Cricut machines, there are thousands of project ideas regarding the Cricut machines. The explanation is clear, there are multiple modifications to add glamor and color to a project with any design, but it's the same concept. Some of the best ideas available that you can build on to bring life into your craft are listed in this chapter below. Take the time to research them and learn from them.

**The basic technique**

Patience is by far the best technique that will allow you to get closer to the ideal project you dream of. Just Relax, take the time to get the job done, and think about innovative solutions. In this way, your projects with the Cricut system will always be more productive. Please take the right attitude about your plans. Also, develop a quizzical mindset asking yourself how you can do things better, you'll find that your projects are running quicker and much more smoothly with these and much patience. Furthermore, when you do it this way, you will have so much more fun!

In the following sections, you can find information about how to improve the quality of the crafts that you make and how to do things more effectively! We have a wealth of information to provide about how the products and fabrics can be expanded and how they can be used as efficiently as possible!

## 5.1: Project ideas for beginners

You will find your Cricut machine with a cardstock, pen, blade, and mat right out of the box. These instruments will get you through the very first tasks of your beginner's projects.

You will no doubt find that your expertise with the Cricut machine will improve very quickly when you understand the Cricut Design Space framework and how the Cricut software works. Such start-up projects are all the right level of expertise for anyone with a Cricut machine, so choose the one you want and get to work!

**DIY Paper Succulent**

Flowers are lovely and make our surroundings incredible. They serve the same purpose, no matter they are live or artificial. Paper flowers and succulents of paper provide our environment with a medium of artificial flora, mainly interior decoration. Undoubtedly, both youngsters and beginners are in love with a beautiful project.

Cricut machine, cardstock, foam mountain belt, different green paint colors, and paintbrush are all part of this super exciting project.

Using Cricut Design Space, design the cardstock. You know how the design list of your library should be modified or selected.

Remove succulent cardstock shapes. Use a dry brush and paint to highlight your succulent leaves. Use the light shade and the medium shade on the tip and edge of the succulent leaves.

Turn your fingers inward, transform the succulent leaves smoothly.

To tie each succulent layer together, use foam mounting tape. Ensure separation of layers as you consider it as practical.

Just position it on top of a craft cup wrapped in a colorful carton to give it a magnificent view. We know that when you start playing with the number of available options for this creation, you will love this project.

## DIY Fabric Bookmark

This project is super easy and a perfect way to start learning skills for beginners. The various colors and designs available for this project and its implementation make this bookmark project particularly amusing. Let's go over how to create your bookmark fabric without much context. You're certainly going to enjoy it.

Take the thickness of your tissue into account for your target size. For each bookmark recommend size is 2.5 "x 7.5" textiles. Fit the fabric on your FabricGrip cutting mat as much as you can.

Use the Design Space to create a 6.70 "x 1.7" thick fusible cardboard. For every bookmark, this should be finished.

Load and cut the fusible cardboard into the machine. To give your bookmarks strength, the fusible cardboard should be thick.

Bring the wrong fabric sides together with clips or pins, and tie it up and downwards.

You are using a pen or pencil to stratify the edges to bring out your fabric bookmark case. To click a bookmark, you have spread out, use iron or EasyPress.

Attach the cardboard in the bookmark case.

Fold open the bookmark case component and press it with EasyPress or iron.

Sew the section not sewed back and cut the two ends. Sew the rest.

Finally, use your EasyPress or pressing iron to press the whole bookmark to make it smooth.

We have aimed to make it easy and straight forward so that you can craft your concepts and materials to life for friends and loved ones and even customized bookmarks. There are various Cricut Library bookmark templates with which you can work.

**DIY Hello Greeting Card**

Remove the protective plastic sheet off the top of your green Cricut cutting mat, and put it aside. Make sure to place it somewhere it won't get wrinkled or broken because this is the layer that you'll place back on top of your mats before you put them back every time. It will preserve their adhesive quality, providing more enduring strength to your mats in your projects.

Line your cardstock up with the upper left-hand grip corner on your mat, with the cardstock's textured side facing upwards. Smooth your cardstock with your hands to ensure that your cardstock does not create holes, wrinkles, or folds.

Once you've lined your cardstock with your mat corner, place the mat in your Cricut machine under the mat guides. Push the mat tightly against the rollers as you press the Load / Unload button at the top of your unit, which is shown by the double arrow.

Open Accessory Clamp A inside your machine and remove the cap from your Cricut Metallic pen that came with the unit. Place the lid on the back of your pen and slip it into place snugly, so you don't lose it when operating. When you have done that, press up gently on the bottom of the accessory clamp A while inserting the pen. Press carefully but firmly into the pin until the pinch covers the little arrow on the pad, and you hear a click. Close the clamp and detach from below your palm.

Now that your machine is loaded and fitted with the right tools, you will find that you are ready to start working. Tap on the menu and select New Machine Setup if you are having trouble locating the project or if Cricut Design Space does not immediately prompt you to continue with this concept. Once again, follow the initial steps before the program brings up the project for you. Additionally, with the keyword "Phone," you can use the project search feature, which will pull up the two-layered greeting card template that we are building here.

To ensure the design is correctly aligned with the materials on your mat, click on the "Make It" button. If this screen tells you that your design will be cut in an area not protected by your cardstock, unload the mat, change your cardstock, reload it and go back to the "Make It" screen, or go back to the design space and change where the design is laid out. If everything is fully mapped out, return the mat to the machine and go back to the "Make It" screen.

Set the dial to the "cardstock" setting on the outside of your Cricut machine to ensure your machine is applying the proper amount of pressure to your blade. This will give you the slickest, most accurate cuts available.

When it seems like all is in order, click the "Go" button. On your Cricut machine, just give it a press until the Cricut C button starts to blink. Your machine must set itself up to draw your design and cut it.

Tap the blinking Load / Unload button once that's complete, and remove your mat from the Cricut machine. Open the Accessory Clamp A, remove your pen, and cover the cap to ensure that your pen won't dry out when working. When your pen has been capped, place it in the front of your machine storage compartment. You'll just remember where it is now.

Flip it face-down onto your work surface to free your work from the mat, so the back of the mat faces you. Curl the corner of your mat slowly back towards you before the cardstock releases from your mat's adhesive surface. Hold the cardstock down onto your work surface with your free hand, adding even pressure to prevent your project from curling when you detach it from the mat.

Fold the cardstock evenly in half, then repeat with the blue paper that came with your machine. Place the paper inside the card until they're both folded uniformly, so it shows through the cut gaps in your cardstock.

Congratulations on completing your Cricut Design Project! You're doing great.

**DIY Wall decals**

Frosty wreaths are pretty wall decals designs and door decorations. They can be used for gifts, sold, and even created for interior design.

Cricut Explore machine, FabricGrip and StrongGrip pads, Cricut Felt, Knife Blade, Rotary Blade + accessories, vine wreath, glue, masking tape, chipboard, and Fabric Brayer are among the materials used for this project.

Allow the chipboard to acclimatize to about 24 hours to avoid bending or warping.

Smooth the StrongGrip mat chipboard using a Brayer for optimal adhesion.

Use masking tape to attach the chipboard edges to the StrongGrip mat. Move the star wheels to the side of the machine, so they don't fall on the chipboard leaving any traces behind.

The Knife Blade will only cut designs inferior to 10.5 "and greater than 0.75." Anything more will damage the blade.

Frequently pause the Cricut Explore computer to test progress by raising the edge of the chipboard.

Use a knife tool to cut the rest to save your StrongGrip mat from wear when the Cricut machine has almost cut through your pattern.

Load the chipboard on top of the StrongGrip mat into your Cricut Explore machine when you're finished with the text design and have a chipboard selected from the list of materials in the Design Space.

To load and cut your design, click the Flashing Cricut button. Remember to pause often to check the progress and remove any loose piece of chipboard, particularly in the snowflakes. It helps avoid stuck parts that could damage the Rotary Blade. Unload the mat and use the knife tool to cut the remaining chipboard to save the mat from wear when it's almost cut through.

Load the second piece of chipboard for the snowflakes and follow step 2 to remove the stuck part and knife blade to finish the segments of the uncut snowflakes.

Use the color of your preference to paint the snowflakes depending on how you want the project to look like at its final appearance.

Set the material to Felt for the felt snowflakes, and use the same process to prepare the felt on the mat for the chipboard, this time FabricGrip mat. Please be careful with the scale of the felt snowflakes, so you don't face the difficulties of taking them out of the FabricGrip pad. Even scrape them gently out of the mat as the cut material will easily crack.

To experience and celebrate your beautifully made and crafted frosty wreath, use the glue to stick them to the 8 "wreath.

**DIY Happy Birthday Card**

Essential supplies for this project include, to your choice, three different cardstock colors, a roll-on tape, and a glue pen. If you think other adhesive forms will work better for you, please feel free to use other alternatively.

Visit the web application of Cricut Design Space and select the option to build a new project. Select "Images" once you're there and check for the word "tag." Choose the shape that looks like a simple gift tag like this: once you've selected this image, you should see the queue at the bottom of your screen filled in.

Now, press the option "Categories" at the top of the screen and select the category "Birthday" before changing your search filter to "Phrases." Select the image of your preference by clicking on it. We picked the one on a wavy banner, which looks like it is.

You can press the green "Upload Photos" button in the bottom corner of your screen after you have made your selection for both pictures. It will connect the images to your design room, allowing you to modify them to suit the design you want to make.

Move the tag picture closer to Cricut Design Space's upper left corner and use the arrow button at the bottom right of the image to scale it to the appropriate dimensions.

The next thing you're going to want to do is to use the circular arrow button to rotate the tag 90 ° so that your Happy Birthday picture matches the tag with a quick resize. But, when you drag the phrase over to your tag, you can find that the text vanishes below the image of the tag. This is not a problem because you can simply click "Arrange" at the top of your screen and pick the option "Move to Front." It will place the phrase above the gift tag so that it is visible.

Now, let's resize the phrase so that it fits on the tag without any problems. Click on the arrow in the bottom right corner and drag it until the outline for your project is adequately sized.

Let's now discuss the color of your images. Although the Cricut machine does not print or influence the color of the materials you are using, it does distinguish where to make its cuts based on the color of the materials in its dock. Place your images in Cricut Design Space to match the color of the cardstock you have on hand to keep your thoughts straight about what cardstock to put where, and to keep your Cricut cutting correctly.

You'll pick a panel on the right side of your screen that shows you every layer of your design. Just click on the image layer that you want to change; color options pop up next to the line. From here, you can simply pick the color that suits the most closely with your chosen cardstock for this portion of your project.

If two layers of your project should be the same color, in the cutting process, you can make it a little simpler by consolidating all of the elements of your design into the same level. Only drag one layer of your layout to the one you want to combine it with and drop it to. It will bring all of them together and keep them in the very same color!

Click "Save," give your project a unique name you can remember, and click "Save," again, until you've got all the elements of your project to look the way you want. Next, click "Make It," to begin the cutting process.

The mat preview screen shows you every step of the cutting process and where the cuts will be made on your materials. Each one of these elements will be divided by color, so you can tell what cuts will be made on your different cardstock pieces.

If you are interested in making several gift tags, simply adjust the quantity of Project Copies to your desired number, then click "Send." This will update your view to show you where the cuts are to be made on the various cardstock colors you have chosen.

Objects in the preview screen cannot be manipulated in any way, so if you still have adjustments to make at this point of the process, simply go back to the Design space, make your adjustments there so that the project is laid out according to your requirements, then return to the "Make It" screen for reassessment and start cutting.

Where everything seems the way you need it is laid out, press the "Continue" button. The next steps of your project will be suggested to you.

At this point in the process, you'll want to make sure that the material dial is set to "Cardstock" on the outside of your Cricut machine, so all the cuts are made as accurately as possible.

Take the first cardstock on the prompt window, and line it up on the mat. Make sure to line up the material, so the grid and the grip on the carpet are square. When done correctly, it should match with the grid corners. Smooth the material with your hands down, making sure that no visible holes, wrinkles, or folds on the material are created.

Place the mat into the unit, sliding it under the guides of the sheet. Hold the mat tightly pressed on the rollers before pressing the Load / Unload button.

Once you start flashing the Cricut C button, press it and watch your computer spring into motion.

Flip it face-down onto your work surface to release your work from the mat, so the back of the mat faces you. Curl the corner of your mat slowly back towards you before the cardstock releases from your mat's adhesive surface. Hold the cardstock down onto your work surface with your free hand, adding more pressure to prevent your project from curling when you detach it from the mat.

After you've finished this step, you'll find that your design parts are all left on the mat and some blanks in the lettering. Using your weeding tool, remove the blanks, and remove the spatula from the mat for your design parts.

Using your Scraper / Burnishing Tool, remove any remaining blanks on your mat, or cut cardstock.

Once your mat is clear, load the next piece of cardstock onto Cricut Design Space as indicated by the screen. Click the Finish button on the Design Space browser window until all the parts have been removed.

When assembling your list, working from the bottom layer up to the top layer will be most comfortable. Keep the Cricut Design Space open to your project so that you can refer to it as you put it in.

Seal the bottom later to the next layer by using your roll-on adhesive tape – or your favorite adhesive media.

Secure the info to your lettering layer using a glue pen — or your favorite means of adhesive. When you have done this, install the lettering onto your tag, and you're all done!

**Customized leather bracelet**

You can also use your Cricut Explore machine with iron-on-vinyl to make your leather bracelets in very convenient steps. You can also use it as a money-making asset or as a gift to some loved one.

The number of designs on the bracelet is as diverse as you might imagine. The materials for this project include your Cricut Explore machine, Cricut Design Space, faux leather, glue, iron-on vinyl foil, craft stick, EasyPress (pressing iron if you cannot lay your hands on EasyPress), bracelet chain. To start: Go to Jen Goode and upload the art set there into your Cricut Design Space.

Start with the design of the mountains and cover undesirable layouts. Ungroup and cover all the unnecessary bits leaving the hills behind.

Choose the mountains and the contour, too. Hide any specifics of the cut, if you wish.

Using the Basic Shape tool, create an oval shape and then cut-out circle from the basic form.

Duplicate this layer on the back of your bracelet for use.

Place the vinyl foil on top of your bracelet, and set it to around 250.

Use the glue to fasten fake leather layers together, usually individually.

Connect the bracelet to the chain and other jewelry. Your bracelet will stand out from the jewelry.

**Customized Planner stickers**

Planner stickers are more like event reminders as they help arrange your events. You need your Cricut Explore Air Machine, StandardGrip cutting pad, printable sticker paper for this project. Navigate to and open your Cricut Design Space.

For example, pick a square or rectangle shape. Alternatively, select a square shape, then use the Unlock Dimension button to unlock its dimensions, and then scale it to your preferred measurements using the arrows.

Use the design features discussed above to design your shape to fill, pick and edit patterns, add overlay(s) where you enter your text, choose the font you want to use when typing your sticker text. Continue the editing until you have the design you require.

To direct the Design Space to submit your built form to the printer, click on the Flatten button at the bottom right of the toolbar. Remember that at this point, you can still edit your sticker by clicking Unflatten on the side of your sticker, editing it, and then clicking flatten again. Clicking the Duplicate button, you can make several copies of your sticker.

Now it's time to put your sticker off the screen. To preview how your sticker will look when you print it, press Make It Button in the top right corner of your screen. The purpose of the preview is to inspect whether you are pleased with the sticker you made.

Press Continue and pick Explore Air from the drop-down menu, then submit to print.

Tap Browse All Materials to pick the preferred material from the Materials list.

Load your mat into your Cricut Explore machine and press the flashing Cricut button to finally cut and pull out your built sticker.

Through experimenting with the various shapes and editing software in the Design Space, you can try out your hands on a variety of different designs. Knowing what you can do with this experience is super exciting.

**DIY Mug Stickers**

Firstly, design your write up in your Design Space. If you're new to Design Space, you might do well to read the clear and concise chapters two and three of this book for your understanding. There's detailed information about how to edit, work with text, fonts, and pictures in those chapters.

The next thing is to follow these steps below to accomplish your goal of having unique expressions on your desired object, a mug in this case.

Measure the width of your mug, so you know the size you want to use in your Cricut Design Room.

Send it over to your mat. Standard Grip Mat is the correct mat for this project. Go to the All Materials button, Choose the material to be used and click it, if it is not listed on the screen. By now, your system should blink.

Cut the appropriate size of the vinyl material to be placed on the sheet. The corresponding size is based on the size of your write-up in your Cricut Design Space.

Place the vinyl on the top left of the mat, which you cut. Ensure that you face the reflective side of the vinyl.

Insert the mat and the vinyl into your Cricut Machine.

Click on the Load button, then press the Cricut flashing button to load and cut your file. Remember that if you don't use the right blade, your Cricut machine will alert you, through your Design Space app. You may be asked to describe which blade you intend to use.

Click the Unload button when finished, and remove your mat from the Cricut machine.

Remove your vinyl from the mat and remove the tiny bits between your letters using your weeding tools. Be sure you don't leave any unnecessary bits of your letters, so it may be unsatisfactory for you to be all your efforts. And take your time to delete them.

Using the transport tape, remove your template from the paper after you have finished extracting the little bits from your letters. Cut the correct transport tape size, so you don't waste it. Also, be sure to peel your conveyor tape before picking up your template. One positive thing about the transport tape is that when it loses its adhesive strength, you can reuse it for other projects.

To get your template, pull the conveyor tape.

Using your scraper, extract any air bubble or extend the edges of your surface onto your desired item like mugs, wine glasses, etcetera.

Finally, remove the conveyor tape from your object's edge to leave your beautiful write-up to your piece.

This is just exciting. You will love to add little items that make your mugs, utensils, wine glasses, and jugs look special. The eye contact is so amazing. As well as coupled with the fact that you can change the writing up and shapes on items, particularly during festive periods (such as Christmas, New Year, anniversaries, a celebration of birthday), and will make you look forward to these experiences.

## 5.2: Project ideas for advanced level

There's no limit to what a Cricut machine can do once you've got the expertise you need to use it. When you start moving into the types of projects that require more skills and abilities, you'll find that you need to branch out to websites that provide their design and cut files that you can use to create more and more innovative stuff.

Because of this, it is often recommended that you look at different online tools for projects that you can do to expand your horizons when it comes to more complex projects.

To give you a few ideas to get you started on where to look, here's a list of some awesome design ideas you can use with your Cricut device to make your design truly special.

**Vinyl designed Wooden Welcome Board**

You will need self-adhesive vinyl, transfer tape, a weeding tool, a knife that is either the TrueControl or another precision blade, your scraper or burning device, a trimmer or scissors, and a wood plaque that is painted or stained to your preference for this project.

Open your browser and navigate to the Design Space at Cricut. Logging in will be your first step if you have not logged in already. This will provide you with access to all of your assets, designs, and items. Once you have logged in, click "New Project." On the left-hand side, select the "Text" option. Type WELCOME into the dialog box next to the text box once the text box pops up onto your screen. Once you have typed that, you'll see the same text filling in the text box.

Now, it's time to pick the font that fits this project best. Choose one that suits your liking. Recommended to this project is a simple, sans serif font. Pay attention to whether the font you have chosen is paid for or not.

Add any additional text you wish in a new line under your WELCOME on your welcome plaque. For this playful, decorative project, it's recommended your family name, or perhaps a fun slogan. Once you have chosen this, redimension it to the same width as your welcome. Both lines of text should be only slightly narrower than your wood plaque's width.

Put both of your text boxes on the same layer, selecting the one that works best for your project with the weight.

Put a certain distance between the text boxes to leave sufficient room for a large monogram. This image will go in between text lines.

Click "Images" and set your Single Layer Images filter, then search for a "monogram" keyword. Select the one you like and click "Insert Images." Place your monogram between your text layers and resize it until it's all in.

Let's curve the WELCOME text, for some added flair. Using a blank form as a guide to this curve can help us evenly line up our letters. Select the shape of the "Circle," stretch it into an oval with the desired trajectory, and place it beneath your WELCOME over your monogram.

Now that you have placed that guide, which you will remove once you have finished lining up our letters, it's time to separate the letters in our WELCOME so that you can individually place them along that curve.

Click on the "Advanced" tab at the top of the screen with the selected text, then click on "Ungroup to Letters." This allows you to place each letter individually along that curve. Make sure the rotation of your letters is adjusted so that the entire word is placed on that curve.

Delete oval placeholder.

Review your text and image and make any changes you may need to make at the last minute so that your design is entirely as per your liking.

Click Select All in the top menu once everything is in order then click "Attach" at the bottom right corner of your screen. The attach option has a small paperclip icon underneath.

Once you've done that, you'll notice all layers are combined into one. To match your material, edit the color of your-now single-image.

Click Save, name the project, and then click Save again.

To commence the cutting process, click "Make It." This will show you where the cuts on the material on your mat will appear.

Set the dial into vinyl on your machine. Line your vinyl up on your mat with the upper left-hand corner of the grip, making sure your vinyl backing is face down. Smooth the vinyl with your hands so that no gaps, wrinkles, or folds in your vinyl are formed.

Once you've got that lined up on your mat, put the mat in your Cricut machine under the guides. Press the mat gently towards the rollers as you hit the Load / Unload button on the top of your machine (indicated by the double arrow).

Press the Cricut C blinking button, and watch your project take shape.

Press the Load / Unload button to release your mat from the machine once the material is fully cut. Make an L shaped cut around your design using a precision blade to release most of the excess vinyl from the mat. Roll up and save that excess for later use.

Burnish the design with your scraper tool before weeding. This will help your design elements stay stuck while you weed at the carrier sheet.

Now hold the weeding tool at a slight angle, hook around your design onto the clear vinyl and gently pull up the pieces you don't need. They can be collected to the side or in the trash in a bin. Once all of the small negative pieces of vinyl have been removed, you can remove the bigger sheet of vinyl around your design.

In the upper left corner, grasp the vinyl, pull back gently, and slowly continue to pull down diagonally towards the lower right corner. Watch for any pieces of your design which stick to the clear vinyl that you remove. You can gently guide those pieces of your model back down onto the carrier sheet using the back of your weeding hook.

Once all that is left at the elements of your design on your carrier sheet, it's time to cut the transfer tape! Place the transmission tape carefully over the entire design. Do your best to avoid bubbles but do no harm to a couple here and there!

Use your scraper tool to burn your design thoroughly into the transfer tape, then peel the carrier sheet away from the transfer tape. This will leave your design stuck to the vinyl transfer tape, with your vinyl adhesive side exposed.

Place your vinyl design gently onto your plaque. Make sure to center it entirely before allowing the adhesive to touch the plaque surface. Use your scraper to burn your design to the surface of your plaque, once you have it lined up exactly where you want it.

Now, peel the transfer tape diagonally down from the upper left corner towards the lower right-hand corner. If any of your design pieces try to come in with your transfer tape, just lay it down, burn it again, then resume peeling.

It's done, and you should now be proudly displaying your vinyl creation on the front of your wooden monument.

**Custom designed Graphic T-shirt**

Among the projects you can do with your Cricut machine, this one is the most fun to do associated with different creative expressions in it, and the fact that it is a business concept that spins money on makes it even more special. And as you go through that step-by-step approach, you'll know how fun this is. Let's begin the step-by-step procedure: open a new project on your canvas Click Templates to view your projects. There are various T-shirt designs under Templates, including Classic T-shirt, V-neck T-shirt, Wide Neck T-shirt, and so on. Click any you prefer.

You can change the color in the top corner of your screen by using the toolbar. That will help you to picture your design accurately. So, change the color to black if you're using a black T-shirt.

Click Images to get an image onto the T-shirt. Type the text in the top right corner of the search box, which defines your model. Unicorn, for example. Use the filter to thin your search, click on Printables, then click on your favorite Unicorn image and insert it into your Canvas.

If you cannot find an image that suits you, there is another viable substitute; Google. Navigate to Google and search for unicorn, select images, and you can choose from a lot of them. Click it right and save it to your device. The only problem with this method is that it is for personal use only if you want to sell it, then you will need a commercial license to do so. It is super simple to use your downloaded image in your Canvas: Click Upload Click Upload Image.

Search and open the image that's downloaded.

Click Setup.

Click Next.

Clean your image of the unicorn.

Click the Preview button to view your image of the final cut.

Click Next.

Select Pictures to Print and Cut and then click Save.

Choose the image you've just uploaded to the library and then click Insert images.

You can print your custom image without using the designed images in the library or downloading online if you wish. How you do this is very simple: Click on the Shapes button.

Choose whichever image you choose, for example, by heart.

Take the image and resize it to 6.5 "or less over the T-shirt.

Go to the menu, Fill, and choose the print option.

Fill your shapes on the Design Space with different patterns by clicking on the Grey button at the top left of the window, select patterns from the drop-down menu to display super unusual patterns.

Use and edit any of the images that meet your Design goal.

You can use text to customize your image. Select Text, type the letters, word, or sentence, and then select the font you want

Move and resize the text, word, or sentence over your image.

The images of your Print Then Cut will appear on the panel of the layer.

Redimension the image to fit in a T-shirt. Traditionally, the image size of your Print Then Cut should be equal to or less than 6.7 "x 9.2."

Drag it to your T-shirt's middle.

If you have more than one layer of your unicorn image, then you need to flatten it. To do this, select all the layers in the layer's panel and click Flatten in your screen's bottom right corner.

Delete all layers except the flattened layer by default.

To make sure the first box is set to Cut and the fill box is set to print, go to the LineType menu above the window.

Click "Make It" to display a black box border in the mat preview area.

To move to the Print and Cut page, click Continue.

One of these fabrics can be used: transfer medium for light-colored fabrics, or medium for dark-colored material.

You need to mirror your image to light-colored fabrics. Click on the Edit link in the top left corner of the window to open a new window. Make sure your image is toggled over the new window, and then click Done

You don't need to mirror your image to a dark-colored medium. So, set Off at it.

Click Send to Printer and make sure to enable the Add Bleed option. Click the "Advanced" option to ensure high quality is set, transfer medium type set to the appropriate one and finally click print to send it to your printer.

Recommended to this project is the inkjet printer. Do not use a laser printer, as this project is not compatible. Choose the correct printer transfer medium and load it onto the printer. Put your transfer medium correctly so you won't print on the wrong side.

Return to Design Space now, click Browse All Materials, search for printable iron-on, select your desired transfer medium, and then click Fix.

Place the transfer medium in your mat's left corner, load it onto your Cricut machine, and then cut off your decal.

Weed your printed transfer medium carefully, starting from the external transfer medium around your decal. If you wish to use the light-colored transfer medium, do not remove the sticker from behind. You only remove your decal from the back for dark-colored medium transfer.

Now it's time for your T-shirt to iron-on the decal. There are two ways of doing the iron-on that are subject to the transfer media.

For a light-colored transfer medium: first press the front of your T-shirt, then place the decal on the T-shirt facing you with the backrest. Make sure the decal is positioned in the middle of your T-shirt. Use your EasyPress to gently press the decal on your T-shirt, at 300oC for about 2 minutes. Remove the backing immediately by using the EasyPress for dark-colored transfer medium you finish your ironing: the first thing you need to do is to press your T-shirt, then place your decal on it with your face. Use a tissue paper to cover the decal, set the EasyPress to 300oC, then place the EasyPress over the tissue paper for around 30 seconds. Remove the iron and tissue paper onto your T-shirt to reveal your decal. If your T-shirt is not correctly attached to the edges, repeat the ironing for another 30 seconds. And here, your project ends with a beautifully customized shirt with you, which you can gift someone or make money by selling it.

**Some more Ideas for skilled crafters:**

**3D Wall Art**: Art that pops off your wall and makes a statement to all of your guests of who you are is something people pay much money to have. Put on your wall a little piece of your creative self, and show off your creativity!

**Aprons:** If you're a kitchen enthusiast, your apron is a great way to add a personalized touch to your experience. You can own the kitchen with a character that you love, a funny saying, or just a monogram.

**Banners:** Any occasion with a banner becomes more official. With Cricut, you can use your materials to create a unique flag that will commemorate the opportunity at hand beautifully.

**Beanies:** A knit cap is a great way to keep warm for any outdoor activity that's going to happen during the winter months. Having one on the side decorated with your design is sure not only to elevate the hat style but also to make others wonder where they can get one like it!

**Bumper Stickers:** There'll always be something stylish to occupy the drivers behind you in traffic. Make some fun statements to put on a bumper for you and your friends!

**Business Cards:** It can be so expensive to have business cards cut from premium stock and in unique shapes. Printing your designs with a standard printer on cardstock and cutting out dynamic models are sure to catch the eye of potential clients.

**Coasters:** Coasters can, like so many other things on this list, make such an excellent gift for housewarming or holidays. Everyone could use unique sets of coasters to maintain secure and dry surfaces!

**Coffee mugs:** Coffee mugs in my house are probably the one dish that I will always want more when I see them. They're great for so many things, and you're the perfect addition to any office or kitchen, having unique ones.

**Coloring Pages:** You can download line art using the pen on your Cricut to create coloring pages of any style or theme for yourself or your loved ones! If you have kids coming to visit your family, that makes for a high group activity!

**Doilies:** Cricut's intricate designs allow you to make doilies with so many different materials, colors, sizes, shapes, themes, and more!

**Envelopes:** Did you know that envelopes are made of one continuous piece of paper that is cut, folded, and glued in a particular way? This means you can take any piece of paper you like, print whatever you want, and make an envelope from it!

**Flowerpots:** A vase can be something of a sophisticated piece. However, they can transform into something that suits your decor perfectly with some craft paint and a stencil that you made with your Cricut, or with a decal!

**Framed affirmations:** This is a tough life! Affirmations you can put in your font or style can make all the difference from a personal space in the vibe you get. Jazz up your own and put it all over your room.

**Hoodies**: Sometimes, nothing is more comforting than a pretty thick hoodie. Put your personal touch on a hoodie or carry Leather Accessories around the mark of your favorite characters or phrases: Wrist bands, wallets, lanyards, cash clips, and more. Your Cricut can transform leather sheets into your prettiest, most elegant accessories.

**Magnetic Storytelling Sets:** You can create a set of fascinating stories and jokes on your doors, fridges, or metal tables by printing words onto a set of printable magnets!

**Magnets:** Think outside the box and make your magnetic designs and cut them into unique shapes to put your style on your fridge or doorstep!

**Origami:** Did you know it makes perfect folding lines with the scoring stylus? Use your Cricut to cut an origami template and score, and go nuts!

**Oven Mitts:** Oven mitts and potholders for iron-on decals that show your personality have a perfect place on their back. All your guests will greet the chef Sealing Stickers between these and your apron: raise your letters and other mails with a beautiful sticker that tells everyone the message is lovingly from you.

**Stationery:** making your personalized letter-writing materials, without the prohibitive cost, gives it that extra personal touch.

**Tea Towels:** Tea towels have an infinite number of uses in the kitchen and are very well designed classically. Some towels add your flair!

**Trivets:** It can be as simple to make trivets as buying a single ceramic tile, putting your design on it, and giving it a clear coat. And you'll get a personalized trivet which will save your table from scorching under Wall Clings' hottest dishes: affirmations, designs, icons, labels, anything you want to decorate on your wall, and for your family.

**Wood Decor:** With the rustic aesthetics as popular as it is these days, the wood decoration is returning in such a big way. Get out there and make some of your home's cutest wooden accents, and then invite everyone to show them off!

**Wooden Snowflake Ornaments:** So perfect for the holidays is a winter woodland theme. Besides this, it is every homeowner's dream to have flat, wood ornaments that are easy to store without breaking.

## 5.3: Business ideas for making money with Cricut

Everybody wants to make money, no matter how little, to benefit himself and his family. You can make your dream of being independent and earn some cash come true with Cricut machines. Also, you will be able to satisfy your ambition to do what you did enjoy best and to make super cool crafts. Below is how your beloved Cricut machine will help you make money. You will see, if you look closely, that the projects we've discussed above are part of the business ideas mentioned below and that they help you much to make money with Cricut. You just need to use your skills and your ingenuity, and the machine has to do the rest of your work.

Here are some of the ideas you can use and make money from:

**Wall Art:** Here, there are infinite possibilities. While the show isn't currently airing with Fixer Upper, the farmhouse wall decor is still going solid. There have been more than half a million searches for farmhouse wall art on Pinterest monthly. Don't miss the moment.

**Personalized Decals:** Personalized stickers are perfect as they extend from party to home decor with so many ends. It's a distinction when you deliver customized service that the larger retailers can't compete with.

**Children Focused Wall Decals:** Decorating associated with children happens throughout the year. From birthday parties to baby showers, baby and kid's decoration are a never-ending requirement.

**Wedding Decor and Standouts:** Wedding industry is present and robust. This is no surprise at all. Backyard weddings are on the rise, according to Pinterest. The quest for them has increased by 441%. Everybody's trying to save some money on their marriage.

**Pen Flowers:** Like farmhouse decor, paper flowers are famous at an all-time high with more than half a million monthly searches on Pinterest for it. From Weddings to Baby Showers, they're perfect for all occasions. They are so in demand, no wonder.

**Cricut Cake Toppers** – Customization is key: toppers for cake and cupcake can be the easiest and most cost-effective thing to produce. At kids' birthday parties, parents are still trying to improve their game with all kinds of personalized decor and favors.

**Leather Earrings:** These cool leather earrings do not take any graphic design skills to make at all. Get a bunch of leather swatches from some furniture store near you if you only want to check the waters and use them to make an initial sample.

**Letters:** Letters merit their category because they are super cost-effective to produce, and there is a need for one from birthdays on any occasion to thank yous' for the weddings. What's more, shipping cards just don't get any cheaper.

# Chapter 6: Maintaining Cricut and Tips for its Effective use

Maintenance is essential to everything you own, and also for the Cricut machine. Think about it like this, you've spent all the money on the machine and equipment, and now you need to make sure that you can take care of the machine so it can work as long since it will be expensive to replace. This chapter will help you keep your machine working well for you, so you can continue crafting.

## 6.1: How to maintain your Cricut machine

After a certain time, you will find that some of your projects are in a less than crisp shape. We will outline a troubleshooting and maintenance checklist that you can use to get your Cricut machine back on top.

Listed below are some maintenance tips that you should follow to keep your machine running correctly.

**Be sure your machine has a secure footing:**

It may sound very basic, but it's also more accurate cutting every time if your machine is on a level surface. Rocking or wobbling the machine could result in unstable results for your projects.

Before you move to the next maintenance step, make sure no waste stuck under the foot of your machines, causing instability.

**Reinstall all cable connections:**

Even if your connections work best, remove all your cabling connections, blow into the ports, or use canned air and connect it to the right ports securely. It helps to ensure that all connections converse with one another.

**Clean Your Machine thoroughly:**

Your Cricut machine works hard. Return to the favor by ensuring that the surfaces and cracks are not obscured by dust, dirt, or debris. Adhesive can be placed around the input mat and rollers on the unit, so be sure to concentrate on those areas.

Use air to blast any of small parts and pieces of material or dust which may be formed around the cutting unit, bar, and rollers and mat input if you have a compressed air pump.

**Inspect the blade housing:**

Debris and residue can often be established in your blade housings. Open and remove any built-up materials that can impede rotation or movement.

**Sharpen the Blades:**

A common Cricut maintenance tactic is to stick a clean and fresh foil on your Cricut mat and sharpen it with your blade. Running the blades through the thin metal helps regenerate their borders and give them a little extra strength until it is time to pick up replacements.

Another option is to make a ball of foil, remove the blades from the casing, and insert them several times in the foil ball until you see a shine on edge. You will also get a better understanding of how the blades are sharpened before you finish with them, so it seems more efficient to sharpen a variety of blades in a sitting. Still, reviews are just as good as if the tool will work together for you on a single blade.

**Clean your Cricut mat**

Cricut mat can be cleaned using a variety of different cleaning techniques, depending on their various types:

**For FabricGrip Cricut mat:**

Do not use a scraper tool, unlike other Cricut mats, to remove bits of fabric. The oils on your finger will minimize the adhesive on the surface of the mat.

To clean this pad, use just the Cricut spatula, tweezers, or StrongGrip transfer tape.

This mat should not be washed by cleaning agents like soap and water.

**For other mats:**

Use the scrapper method to remove the remaining materials from your Cricut mat.

Pick an excellent sticky roller and run it over your Cricut mat for smaller residual parts, which are difficult to extract.

Wash your Cricut mat with some gentle detergent and let it dry with the wind.

To clean the surface of your Cricut mat, use a nonalcoholic cleaning wipe.

**Use a Lint Roller for your mats:**

This might sound somewhat unnecessary, but it is a lifesaver that will save you a lot of trouble and maintain the pressure on your pad. Little pieces of dust and dirt will find their way onto your mat as you do more and more tasks. You'll find an abundance of dust, ashes, paper scraps, glitter, cloth, and perhaps more. Since Cricut strongly advises against cleaning your mats to maintain the grip on them, proper care must be exercised to make them last.

This strategy has been claimed by a significant number of crafters who say that it has added weeks to the lives of their Cricut mats. Nevertheless, since Cricut doesn't support any efforts to boost the grip's staying strength on their mats, it's better to stop using this hack before you're sure you'd like a new mat anyway so that if it doesn't perform well, you can get a new one without thinking you've missed something.

**General maintenance tips:**

The blade holder can be another concern. If there's something inside it, then you need to take the blade out of the blade holder, extremely carefully so you don't harm yourself and make sure there's nothing inside the blade holder that can keep it from sliding when it's supposed to be cutting. If you have one, you do need to examine the blade tip under a magnifying glass. If the blade tip is missing or if chipped, you should immediately replace the blade with a new one. If your atmosphere is dust-free but has excess moisture, then you need to keep your pets out of the room and not cut out when there is moisture in the air as well, as it could affect the components of the machine you need to operate correctly.

If the rail has dust where the wheels are behind the head, you will need to use an alcohol swab to clean the rail. Be careful not to have alcohol on the belt behind the rails because it will damage it, and it will not function properly. If you can see dirt on the wheels behind the head, then clean the wheels, and you can push the head manually to the other side and look out for any other objects that may have been tracked there.

If you have found that the cutting strip directly below the tip of the blade will come up with adhesive, wipe the cutting strip down to remove dust and replace the cutting strip and tape if required. Make sure you are following the instructions of the supplier when you do so else you might do even more harm to your machine.

Make sure you wipe the bar behind the cutting bars and remove any dust or rust. You will need a damp alcohol swab to wipe this down for this move, as well as checking the rollers on the piece to make sure they're still clean. You can manually rotate the bar forward or backward, and if the rollers are removable, you can also remove them to avoid the dust and particles. Some cutters have pressure levers, and they manually lower and lift the component. This way, you can make sure that the rollers are directly above the grit rollers because that's where they're supposed to be because, if they are not, that might also cause harm.

Have your machine turned off before you do anything. Disconnect your machine before attempting anything about cleaning or maintenance. Make sure to turn off the power on your machine and turn it down before disconnecting it, so that the machine is not damaged and you are not injured. Also, you'll make sure the connectors are still secure, along with everything else.

Grit rollers are minimal parts of this massive machine, and they can collect stuff very quickly, so you need to make sure they don't have any bits of tape or vinyl leftovers. They are positioned just below the roller bar we discussed above, and you will find them here. You will need to make sure as it won't be advantageous to your machine if they don't catch the mat tightly to push them when you're cutting. It can cause it to miss a move, which can cause bad cuts and tears, so you'll need to ensure they're all clean. Try to ensure nothing is trapped inside of it.

To do so, you'll need to find some tweezers with a sharp point and catch the bits that are trapped inside. You have to push the bar a little bit at a time manually and go slowly. This will also ensure the paper is removed. If you can't get it clean yet, then you can need to use alcohol on a Q-tip to remove any adhesive that remains.

Nonetheless, one of the best things one can do is to make sure that in the first place, you prevent damage. When resurfacing the mats, make sure that you do not have any adhesive on the edges where the wheels come into contact with the mat and stop using tape around the edges of the mat as well, as it is incredibly difficult to remove the tape from the rollers. Take a couple of seconds before you start your project and go through each of these tips so you can make sure your machine performs at an optimum level, and you don't waste resources or materials. This will also mean the project takes less time, and you don't waste your time whatsoever.

## 6.2: Tips and tricks for cost and time efficiency

There are many tips and tricks which you can use for your machine so you can enhance and boost the quality of your work with your projects. Using these tips, you will understand the fundamental tactics on how to keep your machine running for long and more effectively and adequately use Cricut. Here mentioned are some tips and tricks that you can utilize to save time and money while working on a project with Cricut.

This will probably seem like a no-brainer, but it's a useful tip you need to know. Note that after a project, you should not abandon your pen in the machine. You get so interested in what you're doing that you can forget all the supplies and stuff you leave there, but guess what? It'll be ruined the next time you reach it, and you can't use it. Replace the cover to ensure that it doesn't dry out since you don't want to waste them as they can be costly. Many projects promote this tip, as it is so essential.

Why not try a practice first when your machine is ready to use? It is essential because it allows your machine to get used to it. Make sure this is a small project that does not use a lot of resources and is not a waste. You can make your first card with a sample cardstock.

You will need a scoring stylus for many projects. Many people have not been ordering one, and later they say how much they regretted it. You will prevent it if you purchase it immediately. If your machine is included in a package, you can check if the stylus included.

The right tools here are critical, so make sure you have the toolset. It contains valuable resources and can help you with vinyl in particular.

Know your glue. Several people are fans of what is known as tacky glue. When you start placing it, it gives your projects a little space for wiggling. It will take longer to dry. The question is. Maybe you want to try a quicker one if this is something that worries you.

One trick with the advice above is to make them show up from a different layer. If you want them to be one layer. You may do this with items such as pop dots or zots. These are self-adhesive mounts of foam. You can also make small circles with craft foam or carton and then collect them between layers.

You don't have a craft store to get your supplies. They can be very costly in all reality. There are forms to do this (coupons, certain sales), and you can purchase online or through local sign shops. In some cases, some also sell you free scraps. You can print out the color you need when you need something like cardstock and cut out it so you can take it with you.

The app also features free weekly designs. The catch is that they are only free for one week, so you must also be mindful of that.

Place an aluminum foil on the cutting mast for sharpening your blades and cut a basic pattern. It is a way for the blade to sharpen so that it is easier to cut.

If you want your machine to emboss, you need an extension adapter, and the adapter must replace the blade box, then the style inside. Then tell your Cricut machine to start cutting.

You should use an inkjet printer, not a laser when printing and cutting. Inkjet is going to work better.

You can cut the whole item at once in order to make cuts on two separate materials (such as rose and white cards). Only put the designs in different locations of the canvas. Then pick and add everything in the app hit. Place your materials on the mat in the same position to fit and array.

You can use a wide range of extras to support yourself with your machine. The toolset, additional blades, the ink subscription (often free for the first month), the necessary toolkit, and extra mats can be purchased. All these things will lead to the betterment of your designs and projects.

You have the ability to cut your files On the Explore Air. You can also render them free of charge into a cuttable image. To do that, you need to upload a PNG, JPG, SVG, file.

You need to roll the mat back from the material you are cutting if you want to prevent curling. For paper, that's especially true. It gives you a good cut, and it's going to be flat too. You should not pursue this idea, rather than a good one, with a curled project mess.

Customized stencils can be made for clothing. Customized stencils can be produced for fabrics by freezers paper and excellent designs.

Maintain the order of your blades. We have already spoken about using multiple blades for various projects, but it will also help to keep them organized. If required, you can mark them correctly using different colors.

You would only be able to use this system more accessible if you read the cutting guide of materials.

If you need to do so, you can spray your vinyl. For example, you can spray gold with a Rustoleum metallic and spray your vinyl before cutting and then make sure that it is thoroughly dry before cutting.

You can also customize the designs by cutting and contour. Take advantage of these tools and develop the projects.

It can be a lot of fun with your conditions of search. The library's search terms can be exact. You must understand how to scan and generate images. It'll be much easier for you once you get used to it. One example is leaving an S at the end of your sentences. If you have a word like spot and turn it into places, for instance, it can be challenging to produce a lot of results, but keeping the S off might reduce effects to something you can do with.

When you search, use different wording. Try a name or say something like a plant or a garden, rather than just a flower.

Fast up the color sync tool with the right panel by navigating faster. Colors can be seen and drag and fall!

Don't forget the instrument of the hide. Do not forget. The symbol switches on and off to make it easy to cut and get what you need. It also keeps your canvas free, helping ensure you don't lose the images you still want to use for your designs and projects.

Easy instructions are something else you can use, and make sure that you get to them and use them for your benefit so that you can better and more efficiently use your machine.

Make sure the mirror function is set on the screen. Remember that, if you have already placed the function, you do not have to worry about the extra work. You will have to mirror specific projects.

You must also see how you can edit your cut settings for nearly any material. Many people have questions about the way the cutting system is installed or how the machine can cut vinyl and things such as these. You can, however, adjust your configuration for virtually any material and also set depth, blade configuration, and the number of passes from the materials menu that the machine may require. So the first thing you'll have to do is go to the screen and select the material. You can browse all materials from there, and then in small letters at the bottom, you can say material sets, and you can adjust your settings as you need them, and your projects will be much easier to accomplish.

Another good tip is to see how to connect multiple machines at once. Most people don't have more than one machine, but if you do, you might be able to connect both machines through that app because that app will connect to one account, and you don't have to worry about using the wrong design as it will do for you. Regardless of how many machines you have connected to your account, the very last step on the final screen is to select which one of the machines you want to use, so you can always make sure you use the right machine for the right project.

Along the top toolbar, you can also change how the image is filled with the fill tool. This is a new feature that can help with a preloaded pattern, and the scale can also help.

Keyboard shortcuts are also cutting back on time. The buttons themselves may appear on the images, so be sure to look. For example, the delete button would be a copy of control C while deleting.

Save the materials you cut out the most. You can use the custom materials that you can save time on your project because your machine remembers.

Beware of the box. It may have number one on it, and there will be a note next to it that says sold separately if it does. This is something you need to be aware of and will save you from long-term frustration.

Looking at YouTube videos will also help you, and the machine itself website can help. The videos on the machine website usually take about three minutes to complete.

# Chapter 7: Frequently Asked Questions

While using your machine, there are lots of questions seeking answers because you were not part of the engineers who designed the Cricut machine. Such FAQs have been addressed for you, including the most common issues you will be facing during your projects. Just go through them because you may never know when you might encounter them. This chapter will address the most frequently asked questions about the experience of using Cricut, as well as some of the most common issues that arise throughout the crafting process.

## 7.1: FAQs

Here are the answers to some of the most frequently asked questions by the Cricut user community:

**Where can I find images to use for my project?**

It is a marvel that you can upload files from any source so long as you have the legal rights to use this image, as the space for Cricut Design and the ability to house so many different file types is fantastic. The images are removed from Google image search by handcrafting men, so if you sell the design in some way, you'll want to ensure the images are either freely licensed or purchased for sale and use.

**Do I need to buy all my Cricut fonts?**

Cricut Design Space can use fonts installed on your computer when you browse for your fonts. The fonts can be purchased or used for downloading via the Cricut Design Space with little to no problems. Across the Web, too, there is a range of resources for this.

Nevertheless, if you use a font, make sure you have a license to use the font for the reasons you want to use it! Fonts have copyrights, just like images, and can be limited to what you can do with them.

### Why does my blade cut my support sheet?

It could be due to inappropriate seating on the blade in the package, so move the package back, bring the blade into it again, load it up again and try again. It could also be because the content dial is not adjusted correctly. You can plunge the needle right through the whole material and the back if you cut anything very slim but have the dial set to cardstock.

### Why don't my pictures appear right on my mat?

Once you press "Print it," it is likely that your print version doesn't look like anything in Design Space. When this happens, go back to Design Space, highlight all your photos, click "Team," then click "Attach," and all your project cutting needs will be kept right wherever they are.

### I'm just getting started, do I need to buy all of Cricut's accessories right away?

No, you do not need all the accessories at once, and, depending on your Cricut system, you won't ever need some of them. In fact, you can buy tools and accessories here and there with the help of craft books that you probably already have at hand to start buying from your computer! It doesn't require a fortune to spend on equipment and accessories to do your first Cricut craft project.

### Which Cricut machines at compatible with design space?

All the motorized cutting machines they have on the market are actually compatible. It includes the Cricut Explore, Cricut Explore Air, Cricut Explore Air 2, and the Cricut Maker. With the current version of Design Space, you can use all of these tools to build countless projects for each style. The application needs to test the old machines to see if they are compatible as Cricut provides periodic updates that can nullify the compatibility over time.

## How do I use Design Space on My Chromebook?

Cricut's Design Space is unfortunately not currently designed for Chromebook OS compatibility. It is because the need for the application to download the plugin is a significant obstacle to the operating system, but that doesn't mean that there will be no compatibility in the near future.

## Can I use the Design Space on more than one device?

Sure, all designs, components, fonts, transactions, and photos are accessible via any internet-connected device and your account credentials, thanks to the web-based and club-based features of Cricut. You can start a design during the day and then wrap it up once you're back in your crafting space from any device.

## How many times can I use an image purchased in the Design Space?

Any design asset or feature you purchase from the design space will be yours to use as much as you like when you have an active Cricut Design Space account. Feel free to cut as many designs as you want from your purchased images.

## Can I deactivate or switch the Design Space grid?

Indeed, you can switch grid lines from the design room. Open the Accord menu (three lines stacked at the top left) and select Settings on a Windows / Mac device. The Canvas Grid choices are available, and you can select your preference. You can also see shortcuts in the settings menu. Select the keyboard shortcut to turn off and on grid lines.

## How do I convert to metric units?

To switch to centimeters from inches on a laptop or desktop, open the Account menu, you'll see three stacked lines in the upper left corner, then select Settings. You'll see the options to select inches or centimeters.

## What exactly is SnapMat?

SnapMat is an iOS-exclusive feature that lets you get a virtual preview of yourself. This gives you the ability to align your designs in Design Space so that they fit perfectly with what you put on your mat. This functionality allows you to place images and text over your mat's snapshot so that you can see exactly how your layout should be in the design space.

**What are the benefits of using SnapMat?**

SnapMat gives you the certainty that when you send your design to cut through your Cricut, your images will be placed in. It will show you where your pictures are to be drawn, how cuts are made, and how the text lines up. With SnapMat, you can tell your Cricut to cut a specific piece of a pattern that you've stuck on your mat, write in specific stationery areas, gift tags, envelopes, or cards, and you can get the most out of your scraps and spare materials left from past projects.

**Can I include multiple SnapMat mats at one time?**

SnapMat can snap one mat at a time. If you want to snap multiple mats, you can do so individually, and work that way through your designs. This ensures that each mat is shot correctly and that each one is done accurately.

**What's Cricut Design Space Offline Mode?**

This feature is available exclusively through the iOS platform. This feature allows you to download your items for later use in an offline environment. This is ideal if you plan to work on your designs for a prolonged period of time in a space that doesn't have an active internet connection. You can still work on your designs during that time, without worrying about losing those creative thoughts.

## What is available for offline download?

You can download any element or asset that you own, or you have purchased rights through Cricut Design Space for offline use. This includes images you uploaded from other devices, images, or assets that you obtained through an active membership in Cricut Access. It is up to you to pick what assets you want to make available for offline use.

## How do I save projects that allow me to use them offline?

This step can only be accomplished with an active internet connection, so be sure to download before going offline. Open a project that you want to save for use offline and select the option "Save As." Select the option "Save to this iPad / iPhone," and this will allow you to use the project without any connection at a later time.

## How do I save Offline changes to my projects?

If you are going to work on a project in offline mode, tap "Save," and the file you saved to your device will be updated automatically without having to reselect the option "Save to this iPad / iPhone" if there is no internet connection.

## Can I download images for subsequent offline use?

You may download images to your device for later, offline use, while you have an active internet connection. To do so, open the "Images" screen, select an image, and tap "Download." When this is done, the image label will indicate, and the image will be available immediately, irrespective of available internet connection.

## How many images can I download?

Cricut Design Space does not put a limit to the number of images that you can download in a single day. You can only select 50 images to download at one time, but there is no limit to how many times that process can be repeated in one sitting.

With this feature, when you're offline, you'll have access to everything you need.

**What does the "Select Visible" option do?**

The "Select Visible" option at the bottom of the "Images" screen will select all of the images currently on the screen you are viewing. This feature can help you to quickly group images with as little hassle as possible for fast download.

**Where can I view my downloads from?**

Go to the "Images" screen to view your downloaded images. Once you're there, tap the "Filter" icon, select the "On This iPad / iPhone" option, and all displayed images will be all locally stored images. If you are currently in offline mode, then the "Images" screen will be your default view.

# Conclusion

Cricut is a machine that every craftsman dream of owning. This machine just pushes off all the boundaries from one's imagination and creativity. These machines are a must-have for someone who loves to utilize his creativity and loves to see his fantasies come to reality. The interface provided by Cricut, known as the Cricut Design Space, is so simple that even a non-specialist can use this machine and create beautiful crafts.

The possibilities that the Cricut machine has to offer are endless. Every craftsman, beginner, or professional creates beautiful craft pieces according to their level of expertise regarding the Cricut Machine, and after reading this book, you will not be left out. This book has discussed enough information that You are already ready to go and perform a great artwork of which the world will be proud. So get to work straight away and start creating beautiful crafts. Owning this type of machine is a prime opportunity for many people to develop their expertise in craftsmanship, and it's incredible if you want to venture out and try new things as a crafter because you can add so many new items to your portfolio.

As a result, this machine can literally offer never-ending opportunities for a crafter.

In this book, we've discussed how to set up your Cricut machine as well as the advantages of owning one, and we gave you all the information you need to be able to use it efficiently and effectively.

It is very typical to get overwhelmed when you own a Cricut machine because of all the information. Still, we told you exactly what you need to know to get started and start creating impressive and innovative projects.

There's so much information out there, and the best part is that most of it is free, which means you have more opportunities to get images and things you need to craft, but it also means you get a much bigger chance to get ideas for your projects.

Most people don't even know where to get information about their machine or the items they can use to start crafting, but this book has all the information you need from describing the Cricut machine's most basic function to reflecting ideas for experienced users. We have also shown you that once you have the required skills and the right resources, you can cut even more with the Cricut machines, so you are aware of this as well. In this way, we've made sure you can never forget exactly what you can cut using this machine. However, if you're ever confused, there's a whole chapter in this book on how to set up your machine and how to set up your design space. We have also included some helpful hints and tips to make sure you have some great ideas on how to make it easier for you to use this machine and the supplies, and you can use all of these tips to your advantage. If you follow the tips you've found in this book, you're going to be able to find supplies easier, keep your mats cleaner, use your machine way better, maintain your machine considerably better, and even gain some amazing storage tips and actually make your craft space a place you can be proud of and feel happy and content while you're working. The ability to do that will help boost both your craftsmanship and your emotions.

This book has covered almost all the essential areas for someone who is just starting to make crafts using Cricut. This book has provided a straightforward approach for beginners who want to have a name in the world of crafting and want their crafts to be the best.

# References

- Design Space FAQ. Retrieved from **https://help.cricut.com/hc/en-us/articles/360009503353-Design-Space-FAQ**
- Cricut Design Space for Dummies. Retrieved from **https://leapoffaithcrafting.com/cricut-design-space-for-dummies/**
- Full Cricut Design Space Tutorial for Beginners – 2020. (2020). Retrieved 26 March 2020, from **https://www.daydreamintoreality.com/cricut-design-space-canvas-tutorial/**
- TOP TIPS AND TRICKS: THE BASICS OF CRICUT DESIGN SPACE. Retrieved from **https://www.everydayjenny.com/top-tips-and-tricks-the-basics-of-cricut-design-space/**
- What is a Cricut & 50+ Things you Need to Know Before Buying one. Retrieved from **https://www.daydreamintoreality.com/cricut-need-know/**

- Cricut Experience. Retrieved from **https://cricut.com/experience**
- Cricut Design Space Subscription Explained. Retrieved from **https://damasklove.com/cricut-design-space-subscription-explained/**

www.ingramcontent.com/pod-product-compliance
Lightning Source LLC
LaVergne TN
LVHW091548100325
805596LV00007B/231